SABINO CANYON

SABINO CANYON

THE LIFE OF A SOUTHWESTERN OASIS

David Wentworth Lazaroff

THE UNIVERSITY OF ARIZONA PRESS
and
FRIENDS OF SABINO CANYON

The University of Arizona Press
www.uapress.arizona.edu

Printed in the United States of America
27 26 25 24 23   9 8 7 6 5

ISBN-13: 978-0-8165-1344-4 (paper)

Cover photograph: fall at the second bridge in Upper Sabino Canyon. © David W. Lazaroff.
Frontispiece: Spring in Upper Sabino Canyon
Dedication: Barrel cactus
Opposite contents: Stones, leaves, and autumn reflections in Sabino Creek
Maps and drawings on pages 6–7, 23, 33, 46–47, and 51 are by Marilyn Hoff Stewart.

Library of Congress Cataloging-in-Publication Data
Lazaroff, David Wentworth, 1948–
  Sabino canyon: The life of a Southwestern Oasis / David Wentworth Lazaroff.
    p. cm
  Includes bibliographical references and index.
   ISBN 0-8165-1320-1 (cloth)
   ISBN 0-8165-1344-9 (pbk.)
 1. Natural history—Arizona—Sabino Canyon. 2. Human ecology—Arizona—Sabino Canyon.
I. Title.
  QH105.A65L39   1991
  508.791'77—dc20
                        92-18057

∞ This paper meets the requirements of ANSI/NISO Z39.48-1992 (Permanence of Paper).

For Cherie

Contents

Preface

Aravaipa, Cave Creek, Madera, Ramsey, Sabino, Sycamore — the great mountain canyons of southeastern Arizona are all focal points of natural beauty and biological diversity, but something sets Sabino Canyon apart from the others: its closeness to a major city. This accident of geography is a mixed blessing, to be sure, but it has given the canyon an especially intriguing history. It has also made Sabino Canyon one of the most familiar natural areas in Arizona today. For many Tucsonans the canyon is an old friend. We are on a first-name basis. On a sunny weekend morning we say, simply, "Let's go to Sabino."

Yet, for all the canyon's familiarity, surprisingly little has been written about it. There are no published scientific inventories of its plants or major animal groups, such as birds or mammals, and only fragments of its history have previously appeared in print. Because of this, I have depended heavily on primary sources in reconstructing the canyon's human past, and in researching its natural history I have often turned to the most interesting "primary source" of all — the canyon itself. Numerous technical publications and conversations with specialists (geologists, biologists, archaeologists, and historians) have contributed to an overview that is as accurate and up-to-date as I

Fallen leaves litter the surface of Sabino Lake in late December.

can make it. I am sure that lovers of Sabino Canyon will find much that is new in these pages.

Sabino Canyon is a treasure, and its greatest jewel may be its biologically rich streamside woodland. Such habitats are endangered ecosystems in the Southwest; only a small fraction have survived the influences of humankind and changing climate in the last century and a half. At least five other important communities of plants and animals are also represented within Sabino Canyon's walls — in effect, the canyon offers us many of the lowland habitats of the Southwest in microcosm. In a similar way, Sabino Canyon's history reflects in miniature our own evolving relationship with this remarkable region. The canyon's easy accessibility adds enormously to its recreational, educational, and scientific value.

After years of studying and photographing Sabino Canyon, I am more impressed than ever by how much remains to be learned about it. It is this sense of the endless potential for discovery that draws me to the canyon again and again. If this book inspires others to make their own discoveries in this beautiful and fascinating place, I shall be greatly pleased.

Upper Sabino Canyon and the distant pine-covered ridges of the Santa Catalina Mountains

Green lynx spider on a prickly pear cactus flower

SABINO CANYON

A Changing Canyon

Tuesday, May 3, 1887. Tucsonans are going about their business on a pleasantly warm afternoon under a cloudless sky.

One hundred and fifty miles to the southeast, in northern Mexico, the ground suddenly lurches, heaving up a scarp over thirty miles long and up to twelve feet high. A powerful ripple in the earth races out in all directions. It rumbles through Tucson less than a minute later, stopping clocks at 2:12, swaying buildings, flinging crockery to floors, shaking plaster from walls. Terrified citizens run out into the streets and are sickened as the ground rolls beneath their feet. Amid the confusion, some look in amazement toward the Santa Catalina Mountains north of town. What they see is reported in the next day's newspaper: "When the quake struck the old Santa Catalina Mountains, great slices of the mountain gave way, and went tumbling down into the canyons, huge clouds of dust or smoke ascended into the blue sky, high above the crest of the queenly mountain. . . . Great boulders, or little mountains, wrested from their seats by the shock, came thundering down into the valley, bounding over rocks and cutting their way through the air" (*The Arizona Daily Star,* May 4, 1887).

Sunlight fills the canyon on an early morning in May.

If anyone had the dubious fortune to be in Sabino Canyon at that moment, his or her recollection of events there has been lost to us. We can imagine a terrifying scene: great blocks of stone breaking loose from cliffs, tumbling end-over-end, crushing cacti, plunging into the creek. But perhaps only a few rocks fell that afternoon in Sabino Canyon. By now nature has healed any wounds left by this episode, and we may never know for certain.

Changes in Sabino Canyon are seldom dramatic. A wildflower grows, blooms, goes to seed. A cottonwood, stressed by drought, drops a dying limb. A flood shifts a rock a few feet downstream. Over a human lifetime, the canyon may seem to change hardly at all.

Photographs taken in Sabino Canyon a century ago show quaintly costumed men and women in places we easily recognize. They are posing on the same boulders on which people sunbathe today. Only the plants in the background have changed: A willow is gone, but another has taken its place a few yards away. Going back two centuries takes us beyond the age of the photograph or even of written descriptions of Sabino Canyon. Yet, as we shall see in a later chapter, there is reason to believe that the canyon's vegetation was subtly different even then. Twelve thousand years ago, at the end of the last Ice Age, the canyon looked very different indeed. Twelve million years ago, there was no Sabino Canyon at all.

The Evolving Landscape

Twelve million years ago, a precursor of the Santa Catalina Mountains already existed as a range of hills, but the enormous forces that were to create today's rugged mountains were just coming into play. The crust of the earth in much of western North America was being stretched, and it cracked into huge blocks edged by steep faults. Over millions of years some of these blocks became mountains, not by uplift as one might expect, but by being left in place while other blocks foundered around them, forming valleys. The result is an odd up-and-down landscape called the Basin and Range Province, which stretches from northern Mexico into Oregon and Idaho, and includes much of western and southern Arizona.

One of the earliest known
dated photographs taken in
Sabino Canyon, June 10, 1890.
The site is easy to recognize
today. *Courtesy Arizona
Historical Society, Tucson:
photo 24377.*

AGES OF ROCK

The banded cliffs of Sabino Canyon have confounded generations of geologists. These beautiful formations are composed of a hard metamorphic rock called the "Catalina gneiss." By the early twentieth century, when geologists on horseback first mapped the Santa Catalina Mountains, studies around the world had shown that gneiss (pronounced "nice") is created when another rock, such as granite or sandstone, is transformed by intense heat and pressure. Supposing that the gneiss in Sabino Canyon had been formed in this way, scientists began a decades-long disagreement about its age and original form. Some proposed that the light and dark bands were relics of layers in ancient sediments. Others suggested that the bands were formed by the melting and recrystallization of granite. There were other theories as well.

In the 1970s a few geologists threw out old assumptions and formulated a startling new theory for the origin of the Catalina gneiss. If they are right — and the last word on this enigmatic rock has yet to be written — the process began nearly a billion and a half years ago. At that very ancient time, when only the most primitive forms of life inhabited the earth, a mass of molten rock cooled deep underground, forming a huge deposit of granite. Much later, only about 45 million years ago, after the dinosaurs had come and gone, another mass of molten rock invaded the still deeply buried granite, penetrating it in great fingers and sheets. Where the Santa Catalina Mountains would later appear, the earth's crust softened and stretched, smearing and thinning the older and newer layers before they cooled and hardened.

The dark bands we see today are the remains of the ancient granite, and the light bands are the younger rock that invaded it.
In retrospect, it is not surprising that it was so difficult to discover the age of the rock in Sabino Canyon's cliffs. It has not one age, but two.

Catalina gneiss

As the ground sank all around the particular chunk of the earth's crust that was becoming the Santa Catalina Mountains, streams carrying rainwater and snowmelt began cutting slowly into its flanks. They bore silt, sand, and gravel into the surrounding basins, gradually filling them with sediments thousands of feet deep. Movement on the faults surrounding the Santa Catalinas mostly stopped about five million years ago, but the processes of erosion are continuing today in Sabino Canyon and in the other canyons of this mountain range.

We can only guess what lived in the Santa Catalinas during the millions of years of faulting that created them. We know that owing to a drying climate something resembling today's Sonoran Desert first appeared during this period. Later, after the Santa Catalinas had formed, this area became warm and moist, almost tropical. Then about two million years ago the climate started to shift between wet and dry. This was the beginning of the Pleistocene, the period of advance and retreat of the great ice sheets in the northern part of the continent. The Santa Catalinas were well south of the ice sheets, but the climate here swung dramatically back and forth between long periods of cooler average temperatures and greater rainfall, and briefer warm and dry periods similar to that in which we live today.

During each dry period the desert expanded, only to retreat when the climate again became moist. Plant remains found in ancient packrat dens near Sabino Canyon imply that fourteen thousand years ago, near the end of the last moist period, Arizona cypress, Douglas fir, ponderosa pine, pinyon, juniper, and oak grew on the canyon walls. When the climate rapidly warmed eleven thousand years ago, these plants began shifting to higher elevations, while desert species began moving toward the canyon from regions far to the south. The vegetation we see in the canyon took shape gradually as species migrated at their own rates. For example, the beautiful vegetation on the canyon walls, so characteristic of rocky slopes in this part of the Sonoran Desert, did not appear all at once. Saguaros had probably reached Sabino Canyon by eight thousand years ago, but foothill paloverdes did not arrive until four thousand years later.

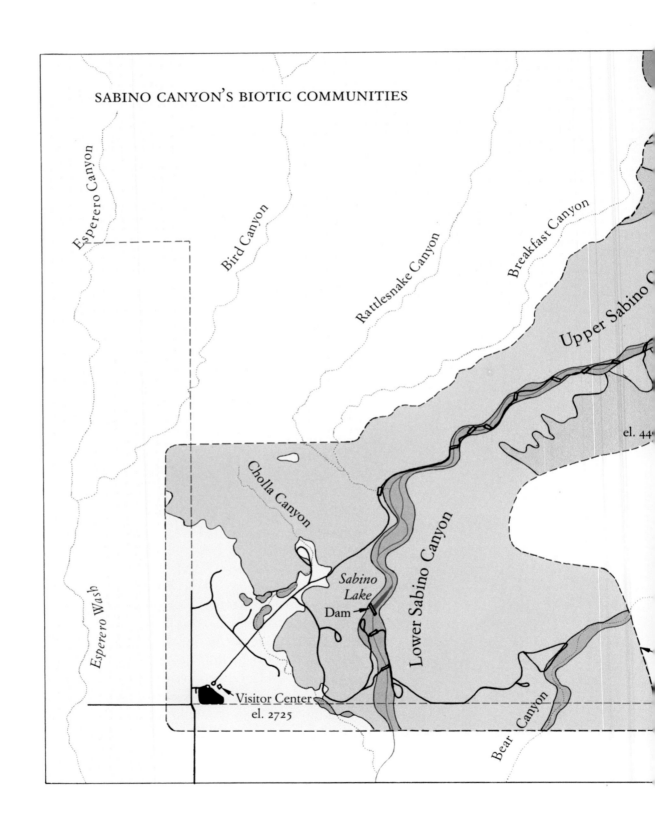

SABINO CANYON'S BIOTIC COMMUNITIES

Espereo Canyon

Bird Canyon

Rattlesnake Canyon

Breakfast Canyon

Upper Sabino C

el. 44

Cholla Canyon

Esperero Wash

Sabino Lake

Dam

Lower Sabino Canyon

Bear Canyon

Visitor Center
el. 2725

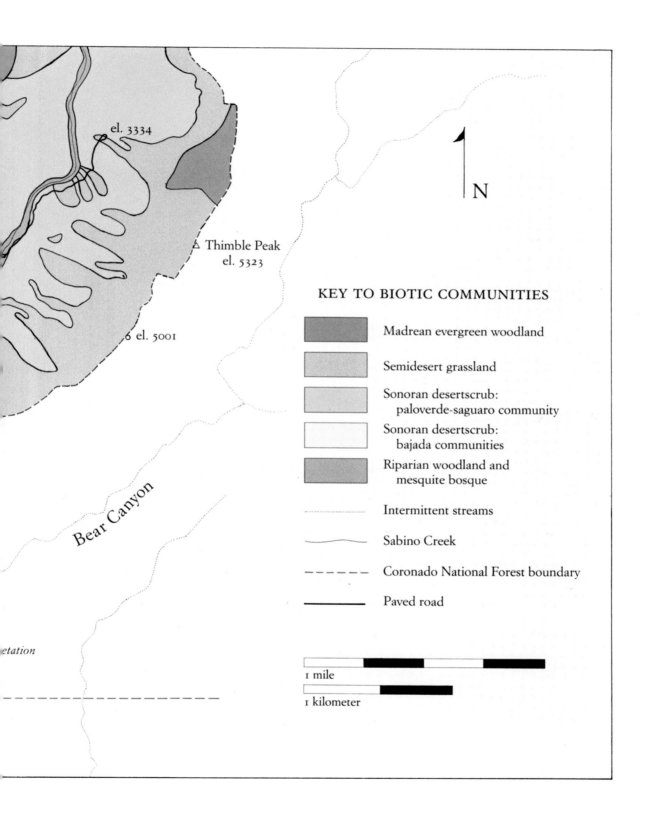

el. 3334

△ Thimble Peak
el. 5323

6 el. 5001

Bear Canyon

etation

N

KEY TO BIOTIC COMMUNITIES

Madrean evergreen woodland

Semidesert grassland

Sonoran desertscrub:
  paloverde-saguaro community

Sonoran desertscrub:
  bajada communities

Riparian woodland and
  mesquite bosque

Intermittent streams

Sabino Creek

Coronado National Forest boundary

Paved road

1 mile

1 kilometer

Biotic Communities

Mountain canyons like Sabino Canyon are "hot spots" of biological diversity. One reason for this diversity is the intricate topography shaped by the forces of geology. Seen from a plant's point of view, a canyon is a complicated patchwork of light and shade, aridity and moisture, warmth and coolness. Each species of plant lives only where it finds the particular set of conditions it needs to grow and reproduce. Animals, in turn, choose their places according to the physical conditions and the vegetation. Ecologists do their best to sort out the wonderful confusion of living things in a canyon by recognizing common groupings of plants and animals, called *biotic communities,* but the boundaries where these communities meet are often hard to define.

All of Sabino Canyon's biotic communities are naturally diverse, but this is only part of the excitement here for an ecologist. Thrusting together so many different habitats in such a small space generates still more diversity by concentrating the resources available to wildlife. In a very real sense, Sabino Canyon is much more than the sum of its parts.

The marvelous pattern of living communities in Sabino Canyon today is a snapshot in a continuum of change. At this moment the climate of the Southwest is the warmest and driest it has been in the last 100,000 years. Thousands of years from now — unless global warming caused by our own species disrupts the ancient cycle — this area will cool again, and the desert will once more leave Sabino Canyon. Millions of years in the future the streams in the canyons of the Santa Catalina Mountains will have finished their work and the entire mountain range will have eroded away.

Meanwhile, Sabino Canyon is here for us to enjoy in all its beauty and extravagant variety.

Sabino Canyon is a rich mosaic of habitats and living communities.

Drought and Deluge:
Life in the Stream

Late afternoon in the second week of July, the canyon is parched after three months of drought. A hot breeze drifts up the desiccated streambed, rustling crisp leaves fallen among the stones, and riffling the few shrunken pools, crowded with agitated fish. A massive cloud looms above the canyon walls, toward the summit of the Santa Catalina Mountains. At sunset the cliffs echo the rumbling of a distant thunderstorm.

The next morning a muddy, leaf-filled torrent bursts into Sabino Canyon. It pours into each empty pool, fills it, and rushes on to the next, banging rocks together and jamming logs between boulders. Cascading down the canyon, the water startles birds into flight and routs an army of grasshoppers, beetles, and spiders from the streambed. By noon the foam-covered current has passed the canyon mouth and is racing away from the mountains toward the dry riverbeds of the Tucson Basin.

Water rushing between boulders in Sabino Creek after spring rains

The stream is the mountain's gift to the desert, but the mountain is a fickle gift-giver. Sabino Creek begins beneath a canopy of firs at an elevation of nearly 9,000 feet, on the shady slopes of Mt. Lemmon. By the time it reaches the desert, 6,000 feet below and ten miles away (as the fish swims), it is a golden tea, steeped in pine needles and oak leaves. In late fall and winter, when melting snow feeds its headwaters, and in spring, when snow gives way to rain, the creek flows generously through Sabino Canyon. But during the hot fore-summer months of May and June, Sabino Creek sinks beneath the sand and boulders and flows mostly underground, appearing only as a broken string of murky pools. The stream is abruptly replenished in mid-summer by monsoon thundershowers, only to dry out again in the after-summer drought of September and October.

This is the pattern, but it exists only in the endless variations created by an unpredictable desert climate. Amid all this uncertainty, life not only persists but thrives in Sabino Creek.

Many flying insects near the stream begin their lives as aquatic larvae or nymphs.

An Underwater "Grassland"

Sabino Creek is far more than a watercourse; it is an ecosystem, with miniature examples of the plants, herbivores, and carnivores found in ecosystems anywhere on earth. In some ways the stream is like an African grassland. Its "grasses" are the algae coating the rocks in a slippery layer, making them hazardous to unwary waders. At times these usually inconspicuous plants bloom into waving green mats.

The "grazers" are mostly aquatic snails, tadpoles, and the immature forms (larvae and nymphs) of flying insects such as midges, mosquitoes, and mayflies. Like grazing animals everywhere, many of these tiny creatures are beautifully camouflaged, blending so well into the background of the streambed that we seldom see them. They graze not only on the algae, but also on a fine stream-bottom detritus, composed of the decaying remnants of plants, aquatic animals, and animal droppings. Leaves falling into the stream from trees on its banks add greatly to this nutritious muck, upon which much of the life of the stream depends.

The "grazers" of Sabino Creek are fed upon in turn by a fierce assemblage of carnivores, the "lions" of the stream. Dull-colored dragonfly nymphs, camouflaged by a growth of algae, stalk or lie in wait for their prey, then snare them with lightning-quick unfolding mouthparts. Fast-swimming predaceous diving beetles chase down their prey. Even their larvae are voracious carnivores; appropriately called water tigers, they grasp their victims in curved jaws, inject a digestive venom, then suck out their juices.

GILA CHUB

One of the great values of the mountain canyons of southeastern Arizona is in providing refuges for plants and animals that are threatened or have disappeared in other habitats. Sabino Canyon is such a refuge for the Gila chub. This unusual fish was once widespread through the Gila River and its tributaries, but habitat destruction and competition from introduced species have reduced its range to fewer than fifteen of Arizona's streams. It is officially listed by the state as threatened.

Fortunately, Gila chub still thrive in Upper Sabino Canyon. Except during the coldest months of the year, when they are mostly inactive and hidden among the rocks, they are easily seen moving about in the stream, the smallest usually in the shallows at the edges of pools and the larger adults in deeper water. They feed on aquatic insects, on other insects that fall into the water, and on algae. They are often mistaken for trout.

The Gila chub is the only native fish in Sabino Creek today. All others have been eliminated by the introduction of exotic species, a serious problem that has plagued native fishes throughout the West. The two most commonly seen exotics in the creek today are the green sunfish and the mosquitofish.

Winter evening light in a rock-lined pool

Crayfish are the "vultures" of Sabino Creek, feeding on the dead remains of other aquatic animals, though they also eat living and dead plants, and sometimes small living animals, such as snails. They have even been seen snatching unsuspecting wasps drinking at the water's edge. A few of the stream's inhabitants have no counterparts in a grassland. The larger fishes and the Sonoran mud turtle occasionally seen basking on the shore are "super-predators" that feed on both the grazers and the smaller carnivores.

Superficial Lives

Sabino Creek's surface is a special habitat in itself, home to a variety of predators competing for flying insects that fall into the water. Schools of mosquitofish patrolling just below the surface belong to this community, as do several aquatic insects highly adapted to life in a world of waves and ripples.

Water striders skate lightly across the surface, their long legs spreading out their weight, keeping them from sinking through the membranelike surface tension layer. They detect their prey by sensing the ripples caused by their struggles and communicate with each other by vibrating their legs, creating special wave patterns signaling aggression or courtship.

Backswimmers are like upside-down water striders living on the underside of the surface. They swim under water by breathing air carried on their bodies — a natural scuba system. They float upward from time to time to replenish their air supplies and press their feet against the underside of the surface tension layer, feeling for the ripples that reveal their prey.

Shiny black whirligig beetles live neither above nor below the surface but straddle the surface itself. Their two eyes are each divided in half, giving them in effect four eyes, one pair looking upward into the air, the other downward into the water. As they race across the water they wrinkle up the surface ahead of them, and their antennae detect ripples reflected back by objects, as bats sense their surroundings and locate their prey through echoed sound waves.

Sonoran mud turtle

Surviving the Extremes

All these creatures must contend not only with each other, but also with the capricious stream itself: the opposite challenges of drought and deluge.

Sabino Creek's inhabitants have a variety of strategies for dealing with drought. Treefrogs, toads, and many insects live in the water only in their immature stages. They can escape by transforming into adults and hopping or flying away — if they time it right. Even many insects that remain aquatic as adults, such as predaceous diving beetles, are able to fly away and seek water elsewhere when the stream dries out.

Animals that cannot leave the streambed face a more difficult problem. Aquatic snails seal themselves inside their shells with waterproof doors formed of their own dried secretions. In spite of this, they may cook if stranded in the sun. Fishes and crayfishes retreat to the few remaining pools, which may contain enough water to last through the drought. As the water level falls, these pools become more and more crowded. If the water disappears, the fish die, suffocating helplessly as their gills dry out, but the crayfish may survive a few days longer by burrowing into the moist sand. Then they face another danger as well: The drying creekbed is often littered with their half-eaten bodies, scattered among the tracks of raccoons. Some aquatic animals do perish during the drought, but enough always survive to repopulate the creek quickly when the water returns.

Spectacular as they may be, floods are briefer events than droughts in Sabino Canyon, and they take a lesser toll. Small creatures, such as snails and many aquatic insects, withstand the rapid current by clinging tightly to rocks. For example, mayfly nymphs have feet like tiny grappling hooks, and flattened bodies that they press close to the rock, staying in a thin boundary layer where the water moves more slowly. Fishes seek shelter between boulders, and crayfishes wedge themselves under rocks with their strong legs. In the long term, most aquatic animals actually benefit from a flood. Nutrients imported from the mountain by flood waters fertilize the plants that are the creatures' ultimate source of food.

CANYON TREEFROG

Visitors soaking up the desert sun on the boulders of Sabino Creek are often completely unaware of smaller creatures basking only a few feet away. These diminutive sunbathers are canyon treefrogs, amphibians that survive by masquerading as stones.

Canyon treefrogs frequently spend the day clinging to smooth stone surfaces a hop or two from the water. Their mottled gray color is often such a perfect match for the rock that they seem to disappear. To complete the deception, they remain immobile for hours at a time, an adaptation called "protective stillness," practiced by many highly camouflaged animals, but which is carried to an extreme by canyon treefrogs — they may not move even when touched.

If discovered, a canyon treefrog has two further levels of defense. As it leaps from the rock it flashes patches of yellow skin usually hidden by its folded legs, startling a potential predator and sometimes fooling it into looking nearby for a yellow animal. Meanwhile the treefrog has turned back into a gray stone or taken refuge underwater. If a frog is caught, it discourages a predator with toxins secreted by its skin. (If you catch one, be sure to wash your hands; if this substance gets in your eyes, it can burn for hours.)

On rainy summer nights canyon treefrogs show another side of their personality, often hopping far from the stream in search of insect prey. Their bleating, sheeplike mating calls are most often heard in the canyon on evenings in April and during the summer monsoon.

DESERT JELLYFISH

To come upon a pool filled with hundreds of miniature jellyfish, rising and falling gracefully through the water not twenty feet from saguaros and prickly pears, is enough to startle even the most experienced desert dweller.

"Freshwater jellyfish" are among the rarest and most remarkable inhabitants of Sabino Creek. Not true jellyfish, they are actually the jellyfishlike *medusa* stage in the life cycle of a little-known aquatic organism. These creatures spend most of their lives in another form, as colonies of minuscule *polyps* attached to submerged rocks. The medusae appear only occasionally, beginning as buds on the polyps, then detaching and floating free. No one fully understands the conditions that cause the medusae to form. In Sabino Canyon they appear unpredictably in still pools during prolonged periods of low water, the only times when they can live and grow without being washed away. They may become as large as an inch across, and seem to be ignored by fish, perhaps because their stinging tentacles make them unpalatable.

Like true jellyfish, these simple animals swim by pulsations of their bodies and capture prey with their tentacles. They feed on minute aquatic insects and crustaceans, and are quite harmless to people.

Freshwater jellyfish

Algae and fallen sycamore leaves

A Well-Connected Ecosystem

One of Sabino Creek's pleasures is that it seems a world apart, a self-contained watery universe set incongruously between desert canyon walls. Yet the stream has strong ties to its surroundings: to the raccoon that feasts on its crayfish, to the tree that shades it from the hot desert sun, to the deer that takes a morning drink, to the mountain that supplies the gift of water itself.

For millions of years, Sabino Creek has joined other rivers and streams in filling a great aquifer beneath the Tucson Basin. Tucson could not have survived through the twentieth century without mining that ancient water supply, a deposit far more valuable than gold. In this way we, too, are connected to Sabino Creek.

The Intricate Tapestry: Life on the Slopes and Ridgetops

A heavy layer of clouds presses down upon the canyon, obscuring the ridgetops. Beneath it, the snow-draped canyon walls bristle with the odd shapes of saguaros, every trunk and upraised arm capped with white. The compact forms of paloverdes, dusted gray, are scattered between the giant cacti. Nearby cliffs and rock outcrops stand out dark and angular, while in the distance the overlapping slopes vanish into a haze of snowflakes.

Close at hand, the desert is a hallucinatory landscape of partially concealed cacti. Elegant hooked spines ornament the white crown on a barrel cactus. Ridges of snow trace the arms of a staghorn cholla; the cactus has been replicated in white, and the original hangs beneath like a shadow. A prickly pear is a constellation of crescent moons, each resting horns-downward on a cactus pad.

A light snowfall dusts the desert's edge, high on a slope in Upper Sabino Canyon.

Such bizarre and beautiful scenes are unusual in Sabino Canyon but not rare. In a typical year (if such a thing existed), it might snow once or twice. It has snowed even as late as April, confounding the desert spring. Snowfall here is part of a desert climate defined not just by heat and drought, but by unpredictability and extremes. More than anything else, it is the extremes that dictate the ways of life of the plants and animals on the canyon's slopes and ridgetops and set the limits to where they can survive.

Paloverdes and Saguaros

Consider the community of plants growing on the sunny north-western wall of Upper Sabino Canyon. From a distance you first notice its largest members: the giant saguaro cactus, with

---

A CACTUS PRIMER

Cacti are the quintessential desert plants. They have dispensed with water-expensive leaves and perform photosynthesis instead with the chlorophyll in their thick stems. Sharp spines reflect hot sunlight, act as windbreaks, and defend their succulent tissues against thirsty animals. In addition to the saguaro, here are several of the more conspicuous cacti growing on Sabino Canyon's desert slopes.

Barrel Cactus
Barrel cacti are pleated like saguaros, allowing them to expand to store moisture. Contrary to myth, there are no reservoirs of clear water inside these plants, only a moist, unpleasant-tasting pulp.

Southwestern Prickly Pear
The rounded pads of prickly pears are not leaves but flattened stems. Their sweet purplish fruits have been gathered and eaten by Native Americans since prehistoric times and are an important source of food and moisture for many desert animals.

Staghorn Cholla
Chollas (pronounced CHOY-uhs) are close relatives of prickly pears, but with cylindrical instead of flattened stems. Flowers on different staghorn chollas vary in color from yellow to red.

Teddy Bear Cholla
The short arms of this species may give it a cuddly appearance, but teddy bear chollas are among the most fiercely spined of all cacti. They grow on the sunniest slopes of the canyon.

Jumping or Chain-fruit Cholla
Spiny segments of jumping cholla stems so easily become stuck to passing hikers that they seem to jump off the cactus and attach themselves. Like the teddy bear, this species is spread when fragments become attached to animals. When these "joints" later are brushed off, they take root.

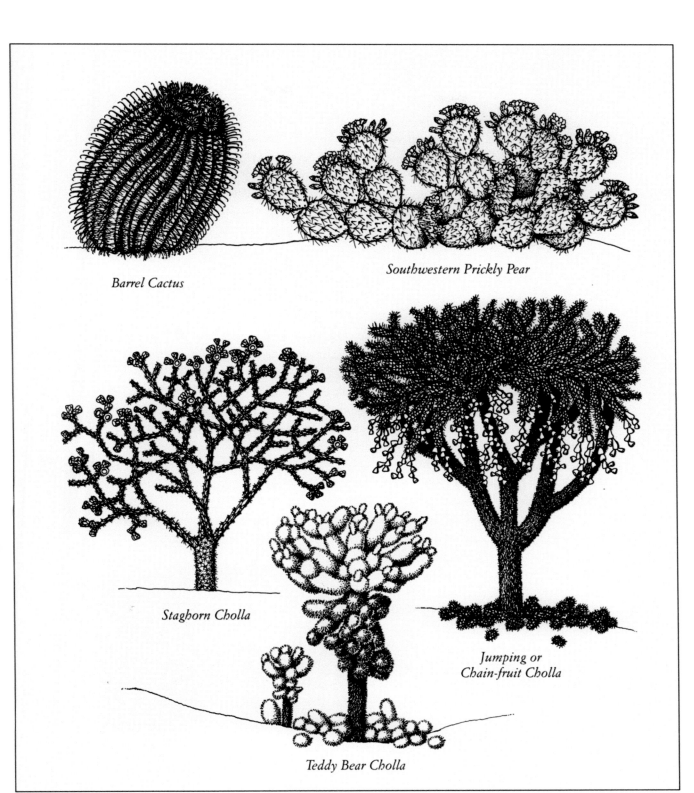

Barrel Cactus

Southwestern Prickly Pear

Staghorn Cholla

Jumping or
Chain-fruit Cholla

Teddy Bear Cholla

its thick trunk and multiple arms — the emblematic Southwestern desert plant; and the foothill paloverde, a small desert tree with smooth green bark, thorn-tipped branchlets, and tiny leaves. These two plants give this particular variety of Sonoran desertscrub its name, the *paloverde-saguaro community*. This striking vegetation, familiar through photographs to people around the world, is typical of the rocky northeastern rim of the Sonoran Desert, the region called the Arizona Upland.

Sabino Canyon's saguaros and paloverdes have very different but equally successful ways of coping with the desert's sparse

DESERT FERNS

When we think of ferns, most of us imagine graceful green fronds on the shaded floors of damp forests. It can be a surprise to discover the diversity of ferns growing on the dry, sunny walls of Sabino Canyon.

Put a delicate forest fern in the desert and it may wilt within minutes. Desert ferns, however, resist drying out in several ways. Many have thick skins, and some are completely covered with woolly hairs that reflect sunlight and shield them from desiccating winds. Still, occasional drying is inevitable. When this happens, the leaves or leaflets of many species curl tightly upward at the edges until only their undersides are exposed to the sun and wind. To further resist evaporation, these lower leaf surfaces may be dusted with wax granules or covered with overlapping scales.

Equally drought-resistant are the spikemosses that cover the soil over much of Sabino Canyon's slopes. Although they resemble true mosses, they are actually more closely related to ferns. During long periods without rain they dry out and appear dead, but soon after a rainstorm they seem miraculously to come back to life. When this happens, the canyon walls themselves change from brown to green.

Star cloak fern

and sporadic rainfall. Like most cacti, saguaros survive by grabbing water when they can and hoarding it for dry times. Their roots are close to the surface, where they soak up rainwater rapidly after summer thunderstorms. Their pleated arms and trunks, filled with spongy tissue, expand quickly to store the water. A thick, waxy skin defends their water reserves against evaporation, and they further conserve their moisture by opening their pores to breathe mainly at night. Thanks to these adaptations Sabino Canyon's saguaros grow, bloom, and set fruit even in the driest years.

Paloverdes, on the other hand, have deep roots, and so tap supplies of water not available to saguaros. In a sense they depend on the soil for their water storage, a far less reliable system than having their own storage tanks. Consequently, Sabino Canyon's paloverdes are more at the mercy of the weather, and in some years only those plants in the moistest sites bloom and set fruit. Unlike saguaros, paloverdes have leaves. These are small, allowing efficient air-cooling on sunny days, and they are jettisoned whenever water is short. The trees then continue to photosynthesize, at a reduced rate, using the chlorophyll in their green bark. (In Spanish *palo verde* means "green stick.")

The saguaro and the paloverde are only the most prominent members of this exceedingly rich plant community. Take time to explore the steep slopes and you discover a bewildering variety of plants of different shapes and sizes: intricately branched cholla cacti, leathery desert ferns, delicate annual wildflowers and robust perennials, disk-stemmed prickly pears, minuscule-leaved shrubs, and many others. Each basic plant design, or *life-form,* is a different set of solutions to the problems of life in an arid land.

If you are used to vegetation composed mostly of a single familiar life-form, such as a forest of trees or a prairie of grasses, Sabino Canyon's paloverde-saguaro community can seem like a botanical garden from another planet. Ecologists explain the extraordinary diversity of life-forms partly by the two seasons of rainfall (winter and summer) in this part of the Sonoran Desert. This complicated climate offers many possible sched-

overleaf:
An ocotillo blooming among the saguaros in Upper Sabino Canyon

ules on which plants can grow and reproduce. Also, the relatively high average total rainfall here—a generous thirteen inches per year in Sabino Canyon—increases the number of potentially successful plant designs. Yet it is not quite enough for the vegetation to become crowded, a circumstance which might allow a single life-form, such as grasses, to squeeze out competitors.

Mapping the Winter Sun

Although plants in Sabino Canyon's paloverde-saguaro community are well prepared for the everyday rigors of heat and drought, many are far more vulnerable to the occasional threat of frost. Evidence for this is written across the shady southeastern wall of Upper Sabino Canyon, most clearly in the distribution of saguaros. Rather than being scattered almost everywhere, as on the northwestern wall, here they are concentrated on the lower slopes, mostly on the down-canyon sides of ridges and rock outcrops. The visual effect is impressive, once you notice it: Scanning the southeastern wall from mid-canyon, you see abundant saguaros up-canyon, to your left, but hardly any down-canyon, to your right.

To understand this odd distribution, you must begin by imagining the shifting pattern of light and shadow in Sabino Canyon through a winter day. On a clear winter morning the light of the rising sun first strikes the top of the northwestern wall, then creeps slowly downward to the canyon floor. In some parts of the canyon it is already midday when sunlight begins climbing the southeastern wall, and then it falls only obliquely, if at all, on the more northerly, up-canyon sides of ridges and outcrops. Many areas on the upper slope stay in shadow until late afternoon. Finally, in the last few minutes of the day, the setting sun shines directly up the canyon, and its reddening rays provide a parting dose of warmth to the down-canyon faces of the ridges.

As dusk falls the bare rocks begin to radiate the day's heat into the clear sky. Scattered across the darkening slopes are

During the cooler months of the year the evening sun warms slopes facing down the canyon.

quarter-inch saguaro seedlings, sprouted in the monsoon rains, scarce survivors of hungry animals and the after-summer drought. Their survival hangs on whether or not the rocks near them contain enough stored warmth to keep them above freezing until they next see the sun.

Seedlings on the northwestern wall have the best chance to survive. Their surroundings were warmed for many hours during the day, and they have an earlier sunrise. But the tiny plants on the southeastern wall experience a longer, colder night. Some growing on the down-canyon faces of ridges survive in the remnant warmth of the previous afternoon's sun. But high

on the slope, and on the up-canyon faces of ridges, in areas that spent most of the day in shadow, frost ruthlessly thins the crop.

Many seedlings not killed outright are too weakened to make it through the next fore-summer drought. The slow-growing survivors will be vulnerable to frost for many years, until they are large enough to store appreciable heat in their own tissues. Eventually, in old age, they will probably succumb to the effects of another frigid winter night.

Paradoxically, it is neither heat nor drought but freezing cold that sets the limits to where saguaros and many other desert plants can grow on the slopes of Sabino Canyon. The convoluted distribution of desertscrub on the cool southeastern canyon wall is a map of winter sunshine. Interestingly, it is precisely here, at its ragged edge, that the desert reaches its peak of diversity: The paloverde-saguaro community on Sabino Canyon's southeastern wall is among the most species-rich plant communities in the United States.

A Shrubby Grassland

A very different sort of vegetation grows beyond the desert's edge, in the coolest pockets and across the shadiest slopes on Sabino Canyon's walls. Plants here must cope with the occasional winter freeze, but thanks to reduced evaporation they have the great advantage of moister soil. The crowded plant community that results, called *semidesert grassland,* is relatively poor in frost-sensitive desert species, such as cacti, but includes a variety of other interesting life-forms.

The word "grassland" may bring to mind the flat, open landscapes of the Great Plains, but the steep grasslands of Sabino Canyon are sometimes so choked with shrubby plants that they are difficult to walk through. Many, such as Wright's lippia and white sagebrush, have pleasantly aromatic leaves, as you discover when you accidentally crush them underfoot. The leaves of others, including hopbush and the aptly named turpentine bush, are resinous and protect them from drying out. Arizona rosewood, a small rounded tree that dots the upper slopes, has thick, leathery leaves, another defense against desiccation.

Desertscrub and grassland communities are interwoven on the southeastern wall of Upper Sabino Canyon.

Sabino Canyon's dense semidesert grasslands are less thorny than its paloverde-saguaro community, but they have their share of sharp objects, too. The hooked prickles of catclaw acacias snag clothing, as do the stout thorns of ocotillos.

The ocotillo ("oh-co-TEE-oh") is one of the most elegant and unusual life-forms in the canyon's semidesert grasslands. During dry periods it looks like a loose bundle of thorny, lifeless sticks, but within days of a rainstorm it covers itself with bright green leaves. Ocotillos often leaf out several times during the year, depending on the vagaries of the weather, but in Sabino Canyon they flower dependably in April and May. Their

THE AGAVE FAMILY

Members of the agave (uh-GAH-vay) family are to semidesert grassland what cacti are to desertscrub: they seem to give the community its special character. These tough, drought-adapted relatives of the lily and amaryllis all have thick, fibrous leaves crowded around short, mostly hidden stems, and grow taller flowering shoots at certain times of the year.

Yucca
Yucca (YUK-uh) moths lay their eggs in the waxy white flowers of this plant, then pollinate them, ensuring that seeds will develop to feed the insects' larvae. In Sabino Canyon yucca is more common in evergreen woodland than in semidesert grassland.

Amole
Anyone who has experienced the short, stiff, spine-tipped leaves of amole (uh-MO-lay) understands why many people call it "shin-daggers." The tender bases of the leaves are eaten by the piglike javelina.

Century Plant
A century plant flowers only at the end of its life (which is much less than a century long). Thanks to its ability to store water in its succulent leaves, it can grow in the drier paloverde-saguaro community as well as in semidesert grassland.

Sotol
The sotol (SO-toll) has ribbonlike leaves edged with sharp prickles. The curved bases of fallen leaves have given rise to the popular name, "desert spoon."

Bear Grass
Bear grass owes its name to its very narrow, grasslike leaves. Fibers from these form the coils in the beautiful baskets made by the Tohono O'odham Indians.

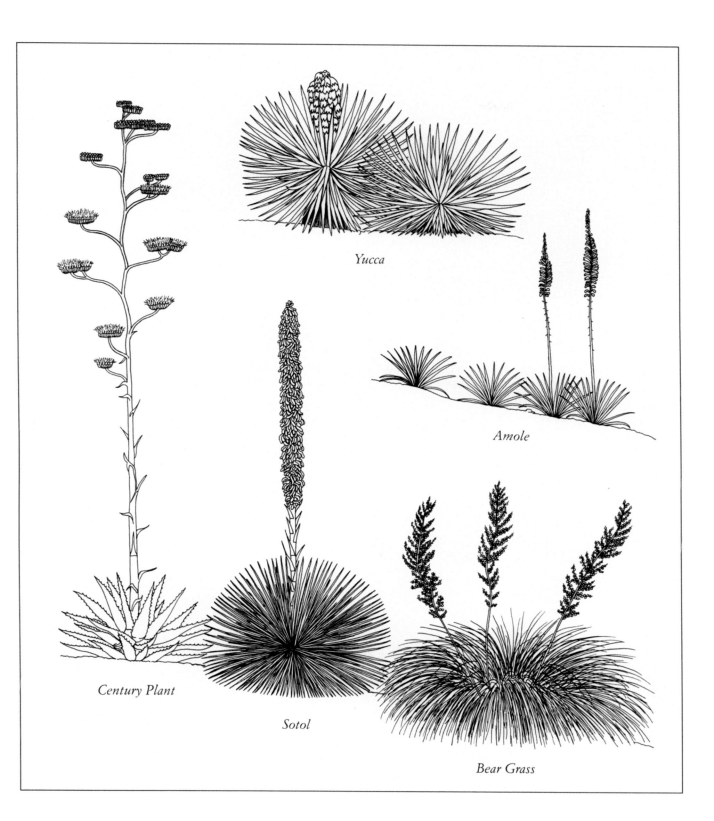

Yucca

Amole

Century Plant

Sotol

Bear Grass

clusters of brilliant red, tubular flowers, waving like flames at the ends of the long stems, are an important source of nectar for the canyon's hummingbirds during the dry fore-summer months. Ocotillos are so well adapted to drought that they thrive in both the desert and grassland communities in Sabino Canyon.

Periodic wildfires, usually started by dry lightning storms preceding the summer rains, are natural if unusual events in Sabino Canyon's dense semidesert grasslands. Most of the canyon's native grasses resprout quickly after burning, revitalized by the ashes, but fire kills many of this community's shrubby plants outright. As a result, areas on the canyon walls that have been burned relatively recently are easy to recognize, as they appear more open and grassy than those that have gone for decades without fire. The patchy mosaic of burned and unburned areas benefits wildlife by adding to the great variety of Sabino Canyon's habitats.

Woodland Outposts

Hidden away on the most elevated ridgetops, nearly invisible from below, are a few open groves of junipers and live (evergreen) oaks. In these places Sabino Canyon barely brushes the lower edge of a beautiful biotic community called *Madrean evergreen woodland*. The mountains of southeastern Arizona are northern outposts for this vegetation, named for its geographic center in Mexico's Sierra Madre Occidental.

Two sturdy trees dominate this community in Sabino Canyon, the Mexican blue oak and the Emory oak. They thrive on the ridgetops where greater rainfall and lower temperatures (and lower evaporation) conspire to make the soil moist enough to meet their needs. Farther down the slopes oak seedlings wither in the fore-summer and after-summer droughts. Sharp-eyed observers may notice an exception that proves this rule: Oaks also grow in semidesert grassland at the bases of cliffs and in drainage bottoms, where the topography concentrates rainwater. (There is another exception, too, as we shall see in the next chapter.)

CLIFF-DWELLERS

The sheer cliffs that rim the walls of Sabino Canyon provide homes for an interesting community of flying creatures, in sites well protected from earthbound predators.

Red-tailed hawks, Sabino Canyon's most common birds of prey, build their large nests of sticks on exposed cliff ledges and also in saguaros and tall trees. They are often seen soaring above the canyon walls or perched on rock outcrops, cacti, or trees, scanning the ground for their prey—mostly squirrels, rabbits, and small birds. White-throated swifts, slender-winged black birds with bold white markings, use their own saliva to glue their nests deep in crevices in the cliffs. They almost never perch like other birds, but spend the daylight hours tearing through the air like feathered missiles, twittering noisily, snapping up insects, and even mating in flight.

In the evening, when these birds return to their nests or roosts, other flying predators emerge from the cliffs. The silent forms of great horned owls can be seen flying overhead at dusk, and their deep hooting calls are heard as they hunt through the night. In Sabino Canyon these large owls sometimes hide their nests in small caves weathered into cliff faces, or take over old ledge nests of red-tailed hawks. Tiny canyon bats, also called western pipistrelles, typically spend the day hanging near the openings of narrow vertical cracks in the cliffs. They begin to fly early in the evening, when the sky is still light, and often leave the canyon to catch insects in the nearby desert.

Great horned owl

CANYON WREN

"A cascade of sweet liquid notes, like the spray of a waterfall in sunshine,"* wrote one ornithologist in describing the song of the canyon wren. This exquisite descending melody, echoing between the canyon walls, is one of Sabino Canyon's most delightful and familiar sounds. The singer may be hard to spot, but with persistence you can usually pick out this tiny red-brown bird perched on a rock high on the slope. A bright white bib makes it easier to find and may serve as a visual signal to other canyon wrens as well.

Canyon wrens are experts at exploiting the canyon-wall habitat. Their slightly flattened bodies and crouched posture allow them to slip easily in and out of crevices as they search for their prey of insects and spiders, and their sharp claws permit them to climb across vertical rock surfaces. Canyon wrens usually build their nests on protected ledges near the ceilings of rock hollows and small caves, out of reach of predators. They often descend to the canyon floor to feed in the lush woodlands along Sabino Creek and to drink.

*Ralph Hoffmann, *Birds of the Pacific States*. Boston: Houghton, Mifflin Co., 1927, p. 242.

The tiny canyon wren is more often heard than seen in Sabino Canyon.

Animals on the Slopes

Verdin

The rugged and varied slopes of Sabino Canyon provide habitats for many kinds of animals. The paloverde-saguaro community, with its wonderful richness of plant life-forms, offers many different sorts of places for birds to nest and feed. Tiny verdins build globular nests of twigs among the stiff branches of paloverdes and glean insects from the foliage of this and other desert trees and shrubs. Cactus wrens, true to their name, embed their larger covered nests among the spiny branches of cholla cacti and poke around for insects on the ground. Gila woodpeckers and northern flickers peck through the waxy skins of saguaros to reach larvae concealed beneath and excavate larger holes for their nests. Surrounded by a jacket of succulent tissue, their young are protected from both the heat of the day and the cold of the clear desert night. When the woodpeckers later abandon their nest cavities, other birds move in, including brown-crested flycatchers, purple martins, and tiny elf owls. Turkey vultures soar above the ridges, teetering on the air currents that rise from the sun-warmed slopes.

Mammals are harder to see on the walls of Sabino Canyon because here, as in most warm desert regions, they tend to be least active during the heat of the day. White-tailed deer wait out the heat on the shadier slopes, then descend in the evening to feed in the lush streamside woodland. Bobcats, common here but not often seen, rest in the shade as well and prey in the cooler hours on rodents and desert cottontails. White-throated woodrats, better known as packrats, conceal themselves by day in their dens, large mounds of twigs and spiny cactus fragments that provide protection from both predators and the weather. Ringtails, catlike distant relatives of the raccoon, prowl the rocky canyon slopes after dark, searching for small mammals and insects.

Mountain lions are only rarely seen in Sabino Canyon, as are bighorn sheep, which occasionally wander into the canyon from their usual habitats on the west side of the Santa Catalinas. Small bands of javelina ("HAH-vuh-LEE-nuh"), or collared

White-tailed deer

The docile black-tailed rattlesnake is sometimes encountered on the rocky slopes, as well as on the canyon floor.

SABINO CANYON'S SECRETIVE NAMESAKE

Dwelling inconspicuously among the fallen boulders that litter the slopes is a fascinating but little-known animal named for this canyon, a snail called the Sabino sonorella. Living sonorellas are rarely seen, as they spend most of their time hidden beneath the rocks, emerging at dusk in wet weather to feed on lichens, mosses, and decaying vegetation. Empty shells found in the open are evidence that feeding snails are often ambushed by predators, and a shell's condition is a clue to the predator's identity. Small rodents bite holes through the tops of shells to extract the snails, but carnivorous beetles and their voracious larvae enter through the front door, leaving the shells intact.

In southern Arizona this and other sonorellas are confined to the mountain ranges that rise above the more arid lowlands. During wetter periods corresponding to the ice ages in more northerly regions, these delicate creatures were able to cross the intervening basins and river valleys, but during drier periods like the present they became isolated in the mountains, where they evolved into many distinct species.

The Sabino sonorella is still evolving, though at a snail's pace. Today this species is found from the Tucson Mountains across the Santa Catalinas into the western foothills of the Rincons. Because the animals are so slow-moving, snails at opposite ends of the Catalinas are almost out of touch and are gradually drifting apart genetically. They are now different enough from each other to be called separate subspecies.

An empty Sabino sonorella shell on a bed of spikemoss

Monsoon rains turn the slopes green in July and August.

peccaries, can sometimes be spotted moving inconspicuously across the canyon walls, pausing now and then to munch on spiny prickly pear cacti.

As one might expect, the greatest diversity of mammals is on the complicated southeastern slope of the canyon, which offers the largest variety of habitats. Three species of squirrels live there. In the early morning large grayish rock squirrels perch on outcrops in the sun, whistling a call that echoes through the canyon. Smaller Harris' antelope squirrels are active even in the heat of the day, periodically dumping their body heat by pressing their bellies against cool rocks or the insides of their burrows. Because of their striped sides, they are often mistaken for chipmunks. Cliff chipmunks, with striped faces as well as sides, prefer the more moderate temperatures of the canyon's semidesert grasslands. A fourth species, the round-tailed ground squirrel, lives on the canyon floor. The presence of four kinds of squirrel in such a small area exemplifies the truly extraordinary diversity of life in this canyon.

The living communities on the walls of Sabino Canyon are like a richly patterned tapestry draped across the slopes and ridgetops. The threads of the tapestry are countless species of animals and plants. Each has its place in the intricate design woven by the interplay of stone, water, and light.

A collared lizard lifts her body from a sun-heated rock and pants to cool herself.

Blooming stalk of a century plant

Streamside Communities: Life on the Edge

The sky is just beginning to lighten above the eastern ridge on a warm July morning. Two great horned owls are calling to each other some-where high on the canyon wall. Their resonant voices echo from the cliffs — distant, diffuse, at the limit of hearing.

Suddenly a raucous chorus erupts from a cottonwood on the canyon floor: Cassin's kingbirds energetically greeting each other and the dawn. A moment later a northern cardinal bursts into brilliant glis-sandi in a nearby willow. Downstream, in a sycamore, a white-winged dove asks loudly, "Who cooks for you?" and soon several others are repeating the question. In a grove of mesquites a curve-billed thrasher whistles sharply twice, then three times, and a verdin fires off a stac-cato sequence of chirps. Nearby, a Gambel's quail utters a plaintive cry, while a cactus wren raspingly scolds its neighbors. Almost inaudibly beneath the din, a mourning dove begins insistently to coo.

A Fremont cottonwood overhanging the creek in Sabino Canyon's lush riparian woodland

Ecologists hear a beautiful theme in Sabino Canyon's dawn counterpoint: diversity. Streamside environments like this one buzz, rustle, and sing with the richest variety of animal life in the Southwest — not only birds, but mammals, reptiles, and in-sects as well. These extraordinary habitats are called riparian communities, from the Latin *ripa* meaning shore or bank, and they are among the greatest treasures in the natural heritage of the Southwest.

The astonishing diversity at water's edge is a delight to naturalists, and a fascinating ecological puzzle. An obsessive ecologist could spend a lifetime trying to comprehend the ways of a single species of beetle, just one member of a community of living things. Understanding why an entire community is species-rich is a problem of a much higher order — it requires contemplating the whole bustling system at once. But ecologists have some important pieces of the puzzle, in the case of the diversity near a stream in a desert mountain canyon:

Mourning dove

1. In an arid environment water is a magnet for animals.
2. The canyon floor is the meeting place of several living communities, each with different resources for wildlife.
3. These communities are enriched by creatures from both higher and lower elevations.

The Lure of Drinking Water

Some animals live near Sabino Creek partly because they need to drink regularly to survive. Mourning doves, for example, must fly to the creek every day, and many save energy by nesting on the canyon floor. Javelina and white-tailed deer commute frequently to the stream from the canyon walls and desert foothills. Raccoons and striped skunks, smaller and less mobile, tend to stay closer to the creek, though they, too, sometimes forage in the nearby desert. Drinking water is essential even to the tiny canyon bats that roost in the cliffs. They can often be seen swooping down to sip from the creek at dusk. By making life possible for creatures like these, the stream adds to the diversity not only of the riparian zone, but of the entire canyon.

However, not all the animals in Sabino Canyon's riparian communities need to drink. Many are desert creatures that have evolved the ability to survive without drinking. The canyon's ground squirrels and packrats can get by on the moisture in the plants they eat, and many desert birds such as curve-billed thrashers, cactus wrens, and Gila woodpeckers can survive on the moisture in their insect prey. Some residents of the canyon bottom, for example, Merriam's kangaroo rat, depend exclusively on the tiny amount of water manufactured by their own internal chemistry. All these species would live on the floor of Sabino Canyon even if the creek were to dry up.

Surprisingly, the availability of drinking water may not be the most important cause of the diversity of wildlife in the canyon bottom. Livestock-watering ponds in the desert produce only the barest hint of the variety of creatures near Sabino Creek. The canyon floor is blessed by a wealth of animal species because it has far more to offer than water alone.

The Crowded Bridge

The floor of Sabino Canyon is not one habitat but many. Several very different plant communities are squeezed together here, in the crowded bridge between the watery oasis of the stream and the arid canyon walls.

A curve-billed thrasher perched on a cholla cactus skeleton

In the boulder-strewn channel is the *aquatic community* of Sabino Creek itself. Lining the channel, and spreading across the stream's narrow floodplain, is a shady *riparian woodland* of tall trees. Above the level of the stream is the remnant of an older floodplain, left behind when the creek cut downward to its present level; on this terrace grows a grove of smaller trees, called a *mesquite bosque* ("BOSS-kay"). Beyond the bosque is the *paloverde-saguaro community* of the canyon walls. Each of these living communities offers its own set of valuable resources to animals.

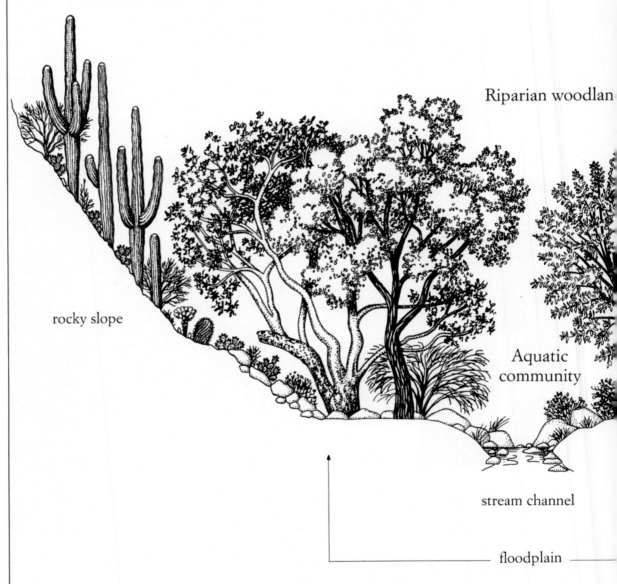

IDEALIZED CROSS-SECTION OF THE CANYON BOTTOM

Paloverde-saguaro
community

Riparian woodlan

rocky slope

Aquatic
community

stream channel

floodplain

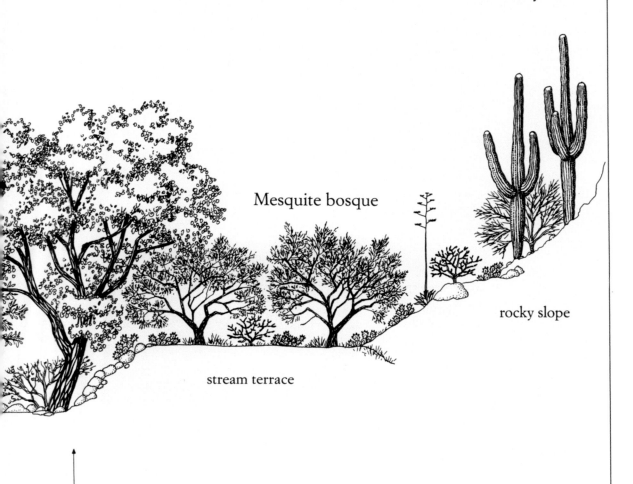

Paloverde-saguaro
community

Mesquite bosque

rocky slope

stream terrace

LIFE-GIVING FLOODS

The word "flood" conjures up images of tragedy and destruction, and there is no doubt that floods can be disasters for human beings who live and work in floodplains. But natural riparian communities have evolved to tolerate flooding, and even to depend upon it, much as pine forests require occasional fires.

In Sabino Canyon the force of the rain-swollen current is seldom strong enough to topple mature trees, but they are often scarred and sandblasted on the upstream side, and their branches may be crammed with debris well above the usual level of the stream. Shrubs and smaller trees are sometimes bent over, partly stripped of bark, and shorn of upstream limbs, but most survive. As in a forest fire, few animals are killed by floods. Most simply leave the floodplain, though some small creatures may drown in their burrows, especially if they are caught during hibernation. Birds fly out of harm's way, and climbing reptiles can take refuge in the trees.

When the water subsides, it leaves behind mud, sticks, oak leaves, and pine cones imported from higher elevations. These rich deposits fertilize plants on the floodplain, and the growth they encourage ultimately benefits riparian animals as well. Floodwaters help to spread the seeds of many plants and to bury them in moist soil where they are more likely to germinate. Sabino Canyon's Fremont cottonwoods and Goodding willows are particularly dependent on flooding for their reproduction. Their wind-borne seeds are short-lived and will sprout and grow only if they fall on moist sandbars left behind by receding spring floodwaters.

Floods may damage the works of man in Sabino Canyon, but they usually benefit its riparian communities.

Life Along the Stream

Some riparian animals depend on Sabino Creek for more than drinking water. Among them are the belted kingfisher, which plummets from a tree branch to spear fish with its pointed bill, and the remarkable American dipper, which walks underwater, completely submerged, searching the creek bottom for invertebrates. Both take food from the stream during the winter but later leave the canyon to nest elsewhere. The black phoebe, a year-round resident, protects its mud nest by attaching it to a rock face overhanging the water. Like other flycatchers and many bats, it often snatches its prey from the clouds of insects that hover above the creek. Black-necked garter snakes are almost always seen close to the water. Graceful swimmers, they prey on tree frogs, toads, fishes, and tadpoles. Raccoons prowl the shore at night, searching especially for crayfish, the closest thing to raccoon ice cream.

Raccoon tracks

Life in the Tall Trees

Many more streamside creatures depend on Sabino Canyon's riparian woodland community for food and shelter, because it adds an especially valuable plant life-form to the mix available to the canyon's animals: the tall broadleaf tree. The ashes, sycamores, willows, cottonwoods, and walnuts along the creek dwarf the paloverdes on the desert slopes, and for good reason. Like any other plant trait, tallness has a function. It is usually an investment to better a plant's odds in the competition for light. Because the desert is dry its trees grow widely spaced and have little need to outgrow the shade of their neighbors. Evolu-

---

THE RIPARIAN "BIG FIVE"

Five beautiful winter-deciduous trees dominate the lush woodland along Sabino Creek. Visitors from the eastern United States are often surprised to find close relatives of trees they know back home, but this is no accident. Despite the desert setting, the moist environment near the stream is not very different from streamside environments in the East or Midwest.

Fremont Cottonwood
Sabino Canyon's great spreading cottonwoods are its largest trees. They are named for the cottony seeds they shed into the wind in the spring.

Bonpland Willow
This common willow of Upper Sabino Canyon is easily recognized by the silvery undersides of its leaves. In the lower reaches of the canyon it is replaced by the Goodding willow, whose leaves are green on both surfaces.

Arizona Sycamore
These lovely white-barked trees are longer-lived than the willows and cottonwoods. Their roots wrap around boulders, anchoring them against powerful flood currents.

Velvet Ash
Velvet ashes light up Sabino Canyon in the fall when their leaves turn brilliant gold. The winged fruits grow only on the female plants.

Arizona Walnut
The nuts of this tree resemble Eastern black walnuts. The graceful compound leaves are larger and have more leaflets than those of the velvet ash.

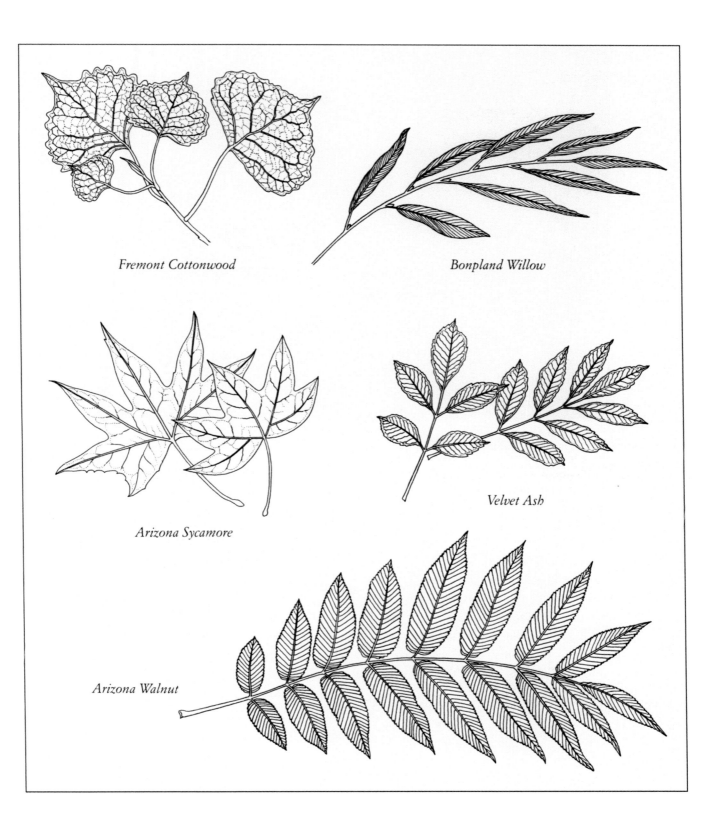

Fremont Cottonwood

Bonpland Willow

Arizona Sycamore

Velvet Ash

Arizona Walnut

A hooded oriole bringing an insect to the young hidden in her pendant nest

tion has programmed tallness into the trees of the riparian woodland as an adaptation to crowding in a moist environment.

The incidental result of this plant self-interest is an enormous boon for birds. A tall tree offers a sturdy framework for nesting and perching, safety from many predators, cool shade, and a large surface of bark and leaves on which to find insects. A lesser goldfinch incubates her eggs in a cup set in the forked branchlet of an ash while her mate forages for seeds in the woodland's shaded understory. A pair of hooded orioles suspend their woven nest from a high sycamore branch and pick insects from the leaves of trees. White-winged doves construct their platform of twigs high in a cottonwood while nearby two young broad-billed hummingbirds are wedged together in a tiny nest on a drooping willow twig. Because tall trees are so scarce in the desert, the slender bands of woodland bordering rivers and streams are the primary breeding habitat for many Sonoran Desert birds, and some nest nowhere else.

Birds are only the most conspicuous inhabitants of Sabino Canyon's riparian woodlands. Sonoran whipsnakes, long and slender as their name implies, climb high into the trees to steal young birds from their nests. Thick-bodied Clark's spiny lizards lie in wait for insects in the tree branches and sometimes become prey for the whipsnakes as well. Black-tailed rattlesnakes hunt rodents in the brush beneath the trees. Like many animals in the riparian communities, all these reptiles also live on the canyon walls but occur in larger numbers here because of the abundant food.

Food draws many mammals to Sabino Canyon's riparian woodlands as well. White-tailed deer and javelina often browse the lush vegetation under the trees but usually retreat from the canyon floor during the hours when the most people are present. They are best seen in the early morning and late evening. During the day rock squirrels climb into the branches of the trees where, surprisingly, they sometimes raid bird nests for eggs and nestlings. At night four species of skunks — striped, hooded, hog-nosed, and western spotted — wander beneath the trees, feeding on a variety of plants and small animals.

Life Among the Mesquites

The mesquite bosque on the stream terrace fills the gap between the lush riparian woodland and the arid desert slopes. Velvet mesquites are beautiful desert trees, distant relatives of paloverdes, with feathery compound leaves and dark, rough bark. Unlike their taller neighbors in the riparian woodland, mesquites are not restricted to the canyon floor — they are scattered across the dry slopes as well. But in the in-between environment of the stream terraces, close to the water yet beyond the danger of frequent flooding, they grow so large and in such abundance as to create a community with a special character of its own.

BIRDS, BERRIES, AND BRANCHES

Nature is everywhere a tangled web, and Sabino Canyon's riparian communities are no exception. A good example is the tight knot of relationships that binds together three inhabitants of the canyon floor. Two participants help each other at the expense of the third in this ecological ménage à trois.

Desert mistletoe plants appear as odd clumps of slender, leafless stems among the branches of mesquites and certain other desert trees and shrubs. They are parasites, living by stealing moisture and nutrients from their hosts. (They may weaken the trees, but ordinarily do not kill them; that would cause their own death as well.) Like all mistletoes, a desert mistletoe faces the special problem of planting its seeds not in the ground, as do most flowering plants, but on the branches of trees. It solves this problem by means of a reddish berry with a gelatinous pulp.

Desert mistletoe berries are relished by many of Sabino Canyon's birds, but most notably by phainopeplas — crested, ruby-eyed, silky black or gray birds that often hide their nests in mistletoe clumps. Phainopeplas feed almost exclusively on mistletoe berries during the winter, when insects are scarce. When the perched birds eliminate the sticky seeds in their droppings, often after flying to a another tree, the seeds adhere to the branches, where they sprout. The minuscule red seedlings seek the dark bark, penetrate it, and "take root" in the living flesh of the tree.

Phainopepla in a velvet mesquite

Greater roadrunners on their nest in a velvet mesquite

For birds Sabino Canyon's open mesquite bosques are like bits of enriched desert. Most of the interesting plant life-forms of the canyon's paloverde-saguaro community, including cacti and many spiny shrubs, can be found growing between the mesquites, providing a great variety of nesting sites. Just as important, the benefits of water a few yards down are passed up the food chains to be received by birds as plentiful nectar, berries, insects, and, for some species, lizards and mice. As a result, mesquite bosques are the preferred breeding habitat for a surprising number of the canyon's "classic" desert birds, including Gambel's quail, greater roadrunners, verdins, and curve-billed thrashers. They are also prime real estate for Bell's vireos, northern cardinals, and mourning doves.

Sabino Canyon's mesquite bosques are literally crawling with interesting reptiles. Small tree lizards are everywhere in the mesquites, but their markings blend so well with tree bark that they are almost impossible to see unless they move. Greater earless lizards hunt insects on the ground. Fast runners, they prefer the more open areas of the bosques and are often seen on trails and roads. Gopher snakes occasionally raid bird nests in the mesquites, but they prey mostly on small mammals, including the pocket gophers for which they are named. Usually, the only signs we see of these secretive rodents are the mounds of dirt with which they plug the entrances to their underground tunnels, sealing out the snakes.

The sweet pods and protein-rich seeds of mesquites are important foods for many mammals in Sabino Canyon, including the Harris' antelope squirrels, round-tailed ground squirrels, and desert cottontails often seen in the bosques during the day. Coyotes prey on all these creatures, especially in the cooler morning and evening hours, but sometimes shortcut the food chain by eating the mesquite pods themselves. Gray foxes hunt their prey in the bosques mostly at night.

The Edge Effect

Some of these diverse inhabitants of Sabino Canyon's floor are closely tied to particular plant communities, but many move freely between different habitats, taking different resources from each. A white-winged dove leaves its nest in the riparian woodland, drinks from the creek, and flies to the desert slope to feast on saguaro fruits. A white-tailed deer walks to the stream from the desert foothills, drinks, nibbles at the green grass under the cottonwoods, then moves into the bosque to pick pods from the mesquites. It is not usually a single community that attracts a creature to the canyon floor but the whole suite of communities, each with different things to offer, all conveniently assembled in a small space.

Ecologists have long recognized the extra diversity in places where different habitats meet, and they have a useful term for this phenomenon: the *edge effect*. The riparian zone is the edge between the desert and the stream, two habitats that could scarcely be more different. An animal on the canyon floor can take advantage of both of these environments, as well as the special resources (such as tall trees, tender green vegetation,

WHIPTAILS

A fascinating group of lizards stalks insects beneath the trees in Sabino Canyon's riparian communities. Named for their long, tapering tails, they are on the move all day, seeking out their prey by sight and smell, pausing only to warm up in patches of sunlight or to dig up insects hidden in the soil.

Canyon spotted whiptails are by far the largest — robust, powerfully built lizards a foot and a half long. Their thick tails leave grooves like bicycle tracks in the soft sand of the floodplain.

The smaller, yellowish-striped, chocolate-brown Sonoran spotted whiptails are the canyon's strangest reptiles, as there are no males, only females. They are the result of a sequence of matings between different whiptail species long ago. Hybrids between species tend to be sterile (like mules) because the genetic mismatch makes them unable to produce normal eggs and sperm. Sonoran spotted whiptails solve this problem by producing an abnormal egg of a special kind, one that can hatch without being fertilized. As a result, all Sonoran spotted whiptails are clones of one original hybrid lizard and as alike as human identical twins.

Both the spotted whiptails live on the slopes as well as in the riparian communities. The third species, the tan-colored western whiptail, lives only in the warmer, more open habitats in Lower Sabino Canyon. On rare occasions it leans back and lopes along on its hind legs, like a miniature dinosaur.

A Sonoran spotted whiptail, heavy with eggs that will hatch into clones of herself

and shade) found only in the narrow transition between the two. The riparian area owes much of its richness to this mating of opposites. It is rich in species because it has so much to offer living things.

Woodland Expatriates

Important as they are, drinking water and the edge effect are still not quite enough to explain fully the diversity of wildlife on the floor of Sabino Canyon. The canyon's riparian communities are also enriched by creatures from both upstream and downstream.

During Sabino Canyon's brief winter, when most of the tall trees have dropped their leaves, a few remain conspicuously green. These are live oaks, and they are mostly the same Emories and Mexican blues that grow in the patches of Madrean evergreen woodland on the canyon's ridgetops. Between the ridgetops and the canyon floor is a nearly oak-free gap of more than fifteen hundred vertical feet.

Two factors combine to create this peculiar pattern: cold air drainage and a perennial stream. On dry, still nights, when the rocks on the canyon walls radiate the day's heat into a black sky, the bare stone chills the air, making it heavy, so that it slides off the cliffs and outcrops and slips silently downward to the canyon floor. By midnight a second, invisible stream is flowing above Sabino Creek. Even more important to the oaks than this cooling flow of air is Sabino Creek itself, which moistens the soil around it. Together, these two influences make the environment of the canyon floor more similar to the highest ridgetops than to the warm, dry slopes in between.

Not only oaks, but many other plants from higher elevations finger downward into the desert on the floor of Sabino Canyon. Interestingly, some animals fit the pattern as well, though the situation is complicated by the mobility of creatures with legs and wings. In cold winter weather rufous-sided towhees sometimes leave their usual homes among the oaks and pines, fly down Sabino Canyon, and take up temporary residence in its

Spotted owls sometimes leave their summer homes in the fir forests of the Santa Catalinas to winter in Sabino Canyon.

riparian communities. Cassin's kingbirds typically nest in tall trees near open habitat. In the Santa Catalinas they find what they are looking for at forest edges, in evergreen woodlands, and in the riparian woodlands of desert canyons. Coatis, long-snouted relatives of the raccoon, wander down from the oak groves to rummage among the sycamore leaves along the creek. Ringneck snakes live in moist mountain woodlands as well as on the floor of Sabino Canyon. These are all woodland creatures, drawn down the canyon not only by the stream, but also by the dense vegetation it nourishes. They are one more piece in the puzzle of diversity in Sabino Canyon's riparian communities.

Interlopers from the Bajada

At the southern end of Lower Sabino Canyon, Sabino Creek leaves the mountains and flows onto a gently sloping skirt of sediments that rings the base of the Santa Catalinas. Ecologists usually call this formation a *bajada* ("buh-HA-duh"), though geologists insist that its upper reaches are more properly termed a *pediment*. The bajada is a sunnier, drier environment than the canyon, and its desertscrub vegetation is simpler and more open than the diverse paloverde-saguaro community of the canyon walls. Partly for these reasons, some of the bajada's animals are different as well.

The situation is particularly remarkable in the case of reptiles. Many of Sabino Canyon's lizards and snakes are completely replaced on the bajada by close relatives. For example, on the bajada, desert spiny lizards take the place of Clark's spiny lizards, zebra-tailed lizards substitute for greater earless lizards, and coachwhips replace Sonoran whipsnakes. A few bajada species, such as the regal horned lizard, have no canyon counterparts. Although the canyon and the bajada do have some lizards and snakes in common, to reptiles they seem to be two very different worlds.

ALIENS

For centuries Sabino Canyon has been repeatedly invaded by aliens, sometimes with the deliberate help of human beings. Not creatures from outer space, the invaders are plants and animals from elsewhere on our own planet, many from as far away as the Old World.

Some are harmless, even amusing, such as the watermelon and tomato plants that appear occasionally in the floodplain. Sprouting from seeds left behind by picnickers, they almost never reproduce.

Others have spread so widely that we are likely to mistake them for native inhabitants. Old World plants such as Bermuda grass, sowthistle, and cocklebur are now abundant in the canyon's riparian woodlands. European weeds like red brome, wild barley, and London rocket have so taken over the floors of bosques in Sabino Canyon that it is hard to imagine what originally grew under the mesquites. All these plants were introduced inadvertently, mostly as seeds and fruits brought in by the wind, in the fur of animals, and in our clothing.

The greatest harm has come from species people have introduced deliberately, in misguided attempts to "improve" Sabino Creek. The loss of the native Gila topminnow is an example of the often tragic consequences of such introductions. Once one of the most common fishes in Southwestern desert streams, it has been replaced in Sabino Canyon and almost everywhere else by the similar mosquitofish, which was imported from southeastern North America to control mosquitoes. Mosquitofish can destroy a population of topminnows in a single season by harassing the adult fish and devouring their young. The Gila topminnow is now a federally listed endangered species.

The thoughtless release of unwanted pets in Sabino Canyon continues to threaten its native wildlife with disease, unnatural competition, and direct predation. Fortunately, Coronado National Forest is doing its best to protect the canyon's natural communities through a special regulation forbidding introducing alien species.

The spiny fruits of the common cocklebur enabled this weedy species to hitchhike to Sabino Canyon from the Old World.

Sonoran whipsnake

Zebra-tailed lizard

Creatures from these two worlds mingle at the mouth of Sabino Canyon. The canyon's mouth is another of nature's wonderful edges: the edge of the canyon environment itself. Here on the canyon floor interlopers from the bajada join mountain woodland expatriates, commuters from the desert slopes, and creatures tied to the mesquites, the cottonwoods, and the stream. In Sabino Canyon's last mile its riparian communities reach their peak of richness.

They sing of their diversity every summer morning.

Portfolio:
Seasons in a Desert Canyon

Visitors to Sabino Canyon sometimes say the Sonoran Desert lacks seasons, but desert aficionados disagree. Not only does the desert have seasons, the seasons are not even particularly subtle. Quite the contrary, they are often dramatic, even spectacular. But they are very different from the seasons elsewhere in North America.

Imagine the four "traditional" seasons, but with the summer greatly expanded and the fall, winter, and spring compressed, and you are well on the way to understanding the climate in Sabino Canyon. Now divide the extended summer into three parts: arid fore- and after-summers bracketing a stormy mid-summer monsoon. You are left with a year of six seasons, but where to begin it?

Many of us think of the year as starting in the spring with the renewal of life after a difficult winter season. In the Sonoran Desert winter is a time of mild temperatures and gentle rains — not a season of stress for living things but a relief from heat and drought. The rains continue intermittently through the spring, and the most difficult time for desert creatures comes later, during the fiercely hot and dry fore-summer months. It makes sense to accept the tradition of the local native people, the Tohono O'odham, and begin the year when the first monsoon

A fall evening in Upper Sabino Canyon

thundershowers break the fore-summer drought.

Add to the complicated seasonal pattern the element of unpredictability, especially in the abundance and timing of rainfall, and you have a climate with both variety and surprise. If anything, Sabino Canyon has more than its share of seasons. And there is beauty in every one.

Monsoon: July through Mid-September

The year opens with a flourish when violent thunderstorms soak the water-starved desert, turning the creek for a few days into a muddy torrent. Toads convene noisily in the evening to mate, and within a week the stream is alive with tadpoles. Soon the brown desert slopes turn startling green as shrubs and trees cloak themselves in fresh leaves. Lizards patrol the moist ground for suddenly abundant insects, while birds feast on the sweet red pulp of bursting saguaro fruits. On the canyon floor morning glories sprout, climb the mesquites, and bloom in the humid dawn.

Sonoran Desert toads mating in Sabino Creek the day after an early monsoon downpour

opposite page:
The light of the setting sun passes through a veil of rain during a July thunderstorm.

A summer evening rainbow

The quiet surface of a pool reflects a nearby cottonwood.

Remains of a crayfish caught in the shallow water by a hungry animal

After-summer: Late September through October

The arid after-summer slips in unannounced. There is only the slightest cooling of the air, the barest softening of the light, to suggest that last week's thunderstorm was the summer's last. Gradually, the canyon grows quieter as summer birds depart for warmer climates to the south. Under the mesquites the green summer grasses begin fading to straw, and the violet morning glories wilt, turn crisp, and drop their seeds. Day by day the stream recedes, then breaks into a chain of still ponds, mirroring the dry desert slopes.

Saguaros and paloverdes on the parched slopes of Upper Sabino Canyon

Fall: November through Mid-December

Gray clouds cover the sun at last and soft rains refresh the desert. Within days the canyon floor is carpeted with the seedlings of winter grasses and next spring's wildflowers. The replenished creek rushes vigorously down its channel, and floating strands of foam twist into chaotic patterns in the pools and backwaters. In the bright, cool days that follow there is a suspicion of change in the foliage at streamside. Then, as November turns to December, the golden peak of autumn color passes in a rush. Soon rafts of fallen leaves are caught between boulders in the stream.

A small waterfall beneath an Arizona sycamore

A patch of sunlight falls on cottonwoods, willows, and sycamores on a cloudy December afternoon.

Winter: Late December through January

As though unsure what a desert winter should be, the weather tries all possibilities. One day cold rain falls gently from a cloudy sky. The next morning fog hangs in the canyon at dawn, then evaporates, leaving the air crystalline. Later in the week squirrels bask near their burrows on a balmy afternoon. Two days later it briefly snows. Through all this the canyon seems subdued, nearly silent except for the steady rush of the creek. On clear evenings the light of the setting sun shines straight up the canyon, reddening the cliffs, and bare tree branches are etched black against the darkening sky.

overleaf:
The canyon is transformed by an early snowfall.

opposite page:
The last light of day falls on saguaro-covered slopes and the snowy peaks of the Santa Catalinas.

A leafless cottonwood against the evening sky

Spring: February through March

Before the canyon can settle into winter, spring declares itself with the bursting of cottonwood buds. The willows and ashes quickly follow, and soon green is everywhere: in the streamside woodland, lacy with new leaves; in the mesquite bosques, lush with grass; on the rocky slopes, draped with spikemoss. Cactus wrens and curve-billed thrashers sing the overture to the nesting season from the tips of saguaros while delicate lace pods and windflowers begin the suite of spring wildflowers. As the days warm, the floral sequence unfolds—fiddleneck, phacelia, globemallow, lupine. By the equinox the sparse garden is at its peak, the first young mourning doves have fledged, lizards are rustling in the underbrush, and clouds of insects and cottonwood seeds are drifting above the canyon floor.

Owl clover

A round-tailed ground squirrel gathering nesting material

A Fremont cottonwood in its new foliage

Fore-summer: April through June

Hot winds steal moisture from the soil, and the spring grasses and wildflowers wither and go to seed. But now it is the real desert's turn to bloom. The garish blossoms of brittlebush, paloverde, and prickly pear turn the slopes yellow, ocotillo flowers blaze red, and mesquite catkins sweeten the air on the canyon floor. Saguaros and the poisonous datura open their white blooms during the short, warm nights. Finally the time for flowering is past, and the canyon begins the long wait for rain. Leaves shrivel as the stream sinks beneath the sand, and days are filled with hot white light and the electric whine of the cicada.

opposite page:
Paloverdes blooming on the canyon wall above the willows and ashes along Sabino Creek

Sacred datura

Hedgehog cactus

An Ancient Oasis:
The Canyon's History

Sabino Canyon's beautiful
stone bridges are a legacy
of the Great Depression.

People may have been part of Sabino Canyon for longer than
saguaros. Twelve thousand years ago, when Paleo-Indian hunters walked into the Southwest at the end of the last Ice Age, it
was still a lush landscape of woodlands, marshes, and lakes,
teeming with horses and now-extinct species of camel and
bison. Large stone spearpoints have been found embedded in
mammoth bones near the San Pedro River, seventy-five miles
southeast of Sabino Canyon, but archaeologists have turned up
scant evidence of the big-game hunters in the Tucson Basin.
We do not know for certain if the Southwest's earliest human
inhabitants ever camped on the banks of Sabino Creek.

When most of the large mammals vanished, perhaps victims
of Paleo-Indian overkill, the people began to subsist on smaller
game, supplemented by wild plant foods. During the thousands
of years that this Desert Archaic way of life flourished (from
roughly 10,000 to 2,000 years ago), the climate warmed and
dried, saguaros and paloverdes moved into Sabino Canyon, and
the Tucson Basin began to look more like the desert it is today.
As a result, mountain canyons like Sabino, with their plentiful food and permanent water, became important to the hunter-
gatherers. Archaeologists have often found their flat grindstones
(*metates*), stone points, and other tools at canyon mouths and

Potsherds left by Hohokam Indians

have tentatively identified a few Desert Archaic artifacts in Lower Sabino Canyon.

Eventually, trade with distant Mesoamerican civilizations brought word of other ways of life to the Desert Archaic people, and they began to plant corn and to live in more permanent settlements. By A.D. 300 the infusion of new ideas had helped to create the sophisticated agriculturists known today as the Hohokam. Over the next thousand years the Tucson Basin's population grew as villages sprang up along the rivers and in the surrounding foothills.

The Hohokam are best remembered today as sedentary farmers, experts in irrigation, but they also kept many of the practices of their Desert Archaic predecessors. They harvested cactus fruits and agave hearts in Sabino Canyon, hunted rabbits and deer there, and used the canyon as a corridor to higher elevations where they gathered acorns and berries. For the first time, human beings began to leave abundant signs of their presence at Sabino Canyon. Today we find rows of stones west of the canyon, remnants of check dams that once caught rainwater and soil to nourish Hohokam crops of corn, squash, beans, and cotton. On the canyon floor there are pits worn in the bedrock and boulders, mortars where the Hohokam ground mesquite beans they gathered in the bosques. And scattered here and there are sherds of Hohokam pots broken hundreds of years ago, some still bearing traces of painted designs.

After A.D. 1200 a small Hohokam settlement near the canyon mouth grew into a large village whose residents farmed the floodplain of Sabino Creek, but within a century the village was abandoned as the population of the entire Tucson Basin shrank. By about 1450 the Hohokam civilization had collapsed. The causes of these momentous changes are a mystery. Archaeologists have suggested climatic shifts, invasions, catastrophic disease, or social strife. Today's Tohono O'odham Indians do not know the explanation. "Hohokam" is an English rendering of a phrase in the O'odham language meaning, simply, "all used up."

On the Frontier of New Spain

Archaeologists know little about this area's inhabitants during the next two hundred years. When Padre Eusebio Francisco Kino rode northward into the Tucson Basin at the end of the seventeenth century, he met Piman Indians, possibly descendants of the Hohokam, living in a string of farming villages along the Santa Cruz River, fifteen miles west of Sabino Canyon. Kino paused to name the village of San Cosme de Tucson and the nearby Santa Catalina Mountains. Perhaps the Pimans were still visiting Sabino Canyon to harvest its many resources, but travel east of the river was becoming increasingly dangerous, thanks to some other newcomers to the Southwest: the Apaches.

The Apache Indians had arrived in this area only centuries before. A nomadic people, they mostly traveled peacefully in family groups, harvesting acorns and pinyon nuts in the mountain woodlands, hunting, and raising small crops of beans, squash, and corn. Some Apaches may well have camped in Sabino Canyon. Unfortunately for the Pimans, the Apaches supplemented this simple hunting-and-gathering economy by raiding their more sedentary neighbors.

overleaf:
Thimble Peak, Sabino Canyon's most prominent landmark, was known as Rock Peak in the first half of the twentieth century.

CYPRESS CANYON

The most basic question about Sabino Canyon's history is also the most puzzling: How did the canyon get its name? No one knows, but there has been no shortage of speculation.

Folk history tells us that the canyon was named after a wealthy, influential cattleman named Sabino Otero, who is said to have owned a ranch at the canyon mouth in the late nineteenth century. This popular story is absolutely true, but of another Sabino Canyon in the Baboquivari Mountains, nearly seventy miles to the southwest.

Because the Spanish word *sabino* is sometimes used as an adjective roughly equivalent to the English word "roan," some have suggested that Sabino Canyon was named for a horse that once grazed there, or for the mottled reddish color of its cliffs. These ideas may seem far-fetched, but no one has disproved them.

There is also an intriguing tradition that Sabino Canyon was named for a plant. But which plant? In Mexico *sabino* is a name applied to small-fruited conifers such as bald-cypress or juniper. The best candidate in Sabino Canyon is a beautiful tree called the Arizona cypress, but most cypresses grow several miles up the canyon, where early Spanish-speaking visitors would have been unlikely to see them. Only a few small, inconspicuous cypresses grow in the lower parts of the canyon today.

But today's Sabino Canyon is not the same as the Sabino Canyon of two hundred years ago. We happen to view Sabino Canyon at an unusually warm and dry time. In the eighteenth century, when Spanish-speaking people may have first set foot in Sabino Canyon, the world was nearing the end of a cooler, moister period, known today as the Little Ice Age. Such a climate probably caused many mountain riparian plants to grow farther downstream than they now do. If there had been even a few mature cypresses in the lower parts of the canyon then, these tall, symmetrical evergreens would have been the most striking trees on the canyon floor.

It seems likely that Sabino Canyon is just one of many Arizona canyons and streams bearing Spanish names for trees — the lovely green *alamos* (cottonwoods), *fresnos* (ashes), *nogales* (walnuts), and *sabinos* that relieved the austere landscapes encountered by early Hispanic immigrants to the arid Southwest.

The largest Arizona cypress in the lower reaches of the canyon today is dwarfed by nearby ashes and cottonwoods.

When Kino arrived, Apaches were already harassing Piman settlements. After the missionaries introduced livestock to the Pimans, the raiding escalated. Spanish soldiers and Piman warriors fought back and by the late 1760s were sometimes chasing the Apaches eastward all the way across the basin. A decade later they began to turn the tables on the Apaches, seeking out and destroying their acorn-gathering camps in the Santa Catalinas and elsewhere. In the 1780s the Spaniards constructed an adobe *presidio* at Tucson, replacing an earlier wooden fort, and began offering free rations to Apaches who would agree to settle peacefully nearby. In 1793 the first Apaches Mansos (Tame Apaches) moved in, marking the beginning of several decades of relative peace.

Even at the height of Spanish rule, enough hostile Indians remained to make travel to Sabino Canyon risky. If Tucson stood on "the rim of Christendom," Sabino Canyon was just beyond the rim, not *tierra incognita,* but a dangerous place nonetheless. The situation deteriorated after the Tucson Basin became part of the newly independent country of Mexico in 1821. The Mexican government could provide neither the reliable rations nor the constant military pressure that had subdued the Apaches, who resumed their raiding.

By this time an important event in Sabino Canyon's history may already have occurred. It is possible that sometime during the late eighteenth century a military detachment rode into Sabino Canyon on the trail of Apaches and gave the canyon the Spanish name by which we know it today.

Early Ranchers

With the ratification of the Gadsden Purchase in 1854, Sabino Canyon and Tucson joined the United States. Two years later the Mexican garrison finally abandoned the old Tucson presidio, and a handful of recent American immigrants celebrated the historic occasion by raising the Stars and Stripes. Among them was a tall Virginian named William H. Kirkland, soon to become a Sabino Canyon pioneer.

In the late 1850s Tucson was not yet a boom town, but things were starting to happen. A stagecoach line connected the village to the outside world, boosting business. Ambitious merchants cashed in, supplying travelers, miners, distant army posts, and Tucson's own growing population. Surely Tucson would soon have its own United States Army garrison — a lucrative new market in itself as well as a source of better protection from hostile Indians. In this optimistic atmosphere, a few brave souls began to risk settling on the rivers and streams east of town.

Around this time Bill Kirkland built a ranch house on Sabino Creek, about a mile south of the canyon. We know almost nothing about Kirkland's ranch, but we can guess that he raised crops rather than cattle there, as an isolated herd might have offered an irresistible temptation to the Apaches. Kirkland made a good living from other ranches and a logging camp south of Tucson, and the outfit he called his "upper rancho" was probably never more than a sideline. But it was the first permanent settlement near Sabino Canyon in five hundred years.

The ranch changed hands several times in the difficult years that followed. When the Civil War broke out in 1861, the army burned its forts in Arizona and headed east to fight, leaving the entire countryside open to Apache raiding. The budding economy collapsed, and many ranchers were forced to abandon their land and take refuge in Tucson. In 1866, after the war, Camp Lowell was established on the eastern edge of Tucson (near the present downtown area), but for many years this tent encampment provided little protection for distant ranches like the one near Sabino Canyon.

In 1873 the old Kirkland ranch was acquired by Tucson's wealthiest entrepreneur, Leopoldo Carrillo, an influential man with interests in mercantile sales, fruit orchards, real estate, and freighting, as well as cattle ranching. That same year Camp Lowell moved east to a site on the Rillito, just six miles downstream from Sabino Canyon, and the soldiers began constructing more permanent adobe quarters. By this time army campaigns and the establishment of reservations had reduced the Apache threat. Nevertheless, the next year one of Carrillo's *va-*

William H. Kirkland, many years after he had sold his ranch on Sabino Creek. *Courtesy Arizona Historical Society, Tucson.*

queros surprised several Apaches killing two head of cattle and barely escaped to report the incident at Camp Lowell.

As soon as Carrillo heard the news, he set out from town with five of his men. A mounted detachment of soldiers was already in pursuit, and Carrillo caught up with them after dark at the foot of the Santa Catalinas. The next morning they began tracking the Indians up Sabino Canyon. The going was rough, and it was evening, high in the mountains, when they finally

ALMOST A RESORT

When city-dwellers were beginning to picnic in Sabino Canyon in the mid-1880s, Leopoldo Carrillo, by then owner of the old Kirkland ranch, was investing heavily in the entertainment of Tucsonans at a site closer to town. In 1886 he opened Carrillo's Gardens, a grand amusement park just south of the city, with exotic trees, artificial lakes, a dance hall, a restaurant, and a menagerie. Now he found himself in the enviable position of owning land on a route to a newly popular mountain canyon. The results were predictable: "Leopoldo Carrillo went out to his Sabino Canyon Ranch . . . yesterday morning, to develop four large springs and run the water to one grand reservoir. This work is done preparatory to building a large hotel and baths, to be ready for the reception of guests next summer. Just what Tucson needs, and indeed, it will be patronized by people from all parts of Arizona . . ." (*The Arizona Daily Star,* August 7, 1888).

Carrillo died two years later without having built his hotel. In a sense he had been ahead of his time. There would not be a resort hotel near Sabino Canyon until nearly a century later.

Leopoldo Carrillo. *Courtesy Arizona Historical Society, Tucson: Buehman Collection.*

found the Indians: twelve Apaches dressed in army uniforms and carrying passes from the White Mountain Reservation. They were on an official army mission to track down a renegade Apache named Chuntz, and they claimed the beef they had with them had been taken from hostile Indians. No one believed them, but little could be done. A month later, a company of Apache scouts, quite possibly the ones who had killed Carrillo's cattle, returned to the reservation bearing Chuntz's severed head.

Pleasure Parties and Picnics

> Visitors to Sabino's canyon, in the foot-hills of the Santa Catalinas, report the place to be indescribably lovely, nature having bedecked the canyon in her forest beauties. As a resort for pleasure parties, the canyon is becoming immensely popular [*The Arizona Daily Citizen,* March 4, 1885].

By the mid-1880s, thanks to the bravery of army forces stationed at posts like Camp Lowell (by then renamed Fort Lowell), the long centuries had ended when travelers in the basin had risked their lives to Indian attack. Tucson had grown from a sleepy frontier town to a bustling city with schools, hotels, newspapers, and a population looking for new ways to spend its free time. City-dwellers discovered the beautiful canyon northeast of town, word spread, and by the time Theodore Roosevelt proclaimed the Santa Catalina Forest Reserve in 1902, Sabino Canyon was already a favorite getaway for Tucsonans.

Most visitors to Sabino Canyon at the turn of the century rode out from Tucson on horseback, or in horse-drawn carriages or wagons. One of the most popular routes was the same road we take today to Upper Sabino Canyon, but then it was a dirt track ending in a picnic ground at the confluence of Rattlesnake Creek and Sabino Creek. Beyond that point a narrow horse trail, called the Sabino Canyon Trail, or Apache Trail, wound its way up the canyon floor toward the high country. Another road led picnickers into the area we now call Lower Sabino.

A light-hearted moment in Sabino Canyon, 1895. *Courtesy Arizona Historical Society, Tucson: photo 57816.*

When Sabino Canyon was a remote oasis at the end of miles of rutted dirt roads, a visit there was a real occasion, often planned well in advance and savored as long as possible. Typical were the day-long outings organized by the Ronstadt family, then already well known for its talented musicians and successful carriage-making business.

The extended family piled sleepily into their wagons before dawn and started down the long dusty road toward the canyon. Along the way they passed the picturesque ruins of Fort Lowell (abandoned in 1891) and later paused in the desert to hunt quail and dove. When at last they pulled under the trees in Sabino Canyon, they cooked a delicious breakfast of wild game, with beans and tortillas prepared in advance. During the

YELLOW AND BLACK GOLD

For a short time near the end of the nineteenth century, people were drawn to Sabino Canyon by something more tantalizing than picnics or water projects. In 1892 a small group of men, including the mining engineer and railroad entrepreneur Col. Charles P. Sykes, staked claims to five gold mines near the mouth of Rattlesnake Canyon. An electrifying announcement followed: "Tucson is on the verge of experiencing one of the biggest mining booms known to the history of Arizona. If the statements of two of the best assayers in the territory are worth anything, the mines in the Sabino Canyon are as rich as any others in Arizona" (*The Arizona Daily Star,* June 19, 1892).

Three years later Sykes enlisted the backing of New York capitalists in forming the Sabino Gold Mining Company, and by 1897 the company had expanded its holdings to ten mines. Sadly for Mr. Sykes (but fortunately for Sabino Canyon), the claims never panned out. Today only short tunnels in the canyon walls remain as evidence of the hopeful enterprise.

The era of oil exploration was even briefer. In 1912 James F. McKale, a high school teacher fresh from Michigan, thought he had struck it rich in Lower Sabino Canyon. Years later he was able to laugh about his short career as an oil magnate. "Somebody had found a little grease on top of the water and I became a millionaire. With two or three other friends who had invested in that oil well, probably to the extent of a hundred dollars, we rented a Packard car . . . to go out there and see our property. It was the most wonderful feeling to know that I was a millionaire. I got over it shortly" (address to the Arizona Pioneers' Historical Society, November 14, 1964, Arizona Historical Society).

"Pop" McKale later made his mark as a popular athletics coach at the University of Arizona.

Col. C. P. Sykes. *Courtesy Arizona Historical Society, Tucson: photo 41045.*

Professor Sherman M. Woodward in 1901, the year he conceived of a great dam in Sabino Canyon. *Courtesy University of Arizona Library Special Collections Department.*

heat of the day they relaxed near the stream, picnicking, exploring, and catching up on family news. It was toward evening when the family finally packed up and headed back. The men made the journey shorter by singing and playing their guitars until all arrived home at eight or nine o'clock, tired but content.

Water for a Booming City

Meanwhile, events had been unfolding in Tucson that eventually would profoundly affect the distant mountain canyon. In the earliest days, Tucsonans had made do with water carried from springs, shallow wells, and the Santa Cruz. After 1882 water had flowed from the riverbed through an iron pipe. Enterprising individuals, realizing that even this new system could not supply the growing city forever, had turned thirsty eyes toward Sabino Creek.

In 1883 Calvin A. Elliott, a former forty-niner and merchant, posted a notice on Sabino Creek, claiming its flow for irrigation, stock watering, and furnishing water to Tucson. By coincidence, soon after that Fort Lowell began having serious problems with its water supply, and in 1886 an army engineer recommended piping water from Sabino Canyon. A few months later the army annexed the lower reaches of the canyon to the Fort Lowell Military Reservation. A heated dispute ensued, but in the end nothing came of either plan. Calvin Elliott was appointed Tucson's postmaster and abandoned his scheme, and Fort Lowell installed a steam-powered pump for one of its wells — a happy solution for the troops at the hot desert post, as the engine could also be used to power an ice-making machine.

These events were only a hint of things to come. In the last years of the century Tucsonans devised increasingly elaborate schemes for bringing the waters of Sabino Creek to Tucson, but none were carried out. Then, in 1901, Sherman M. Woodward, a young professor in the Department of Mathematics and Mechanics at the University of Arizona, formulated a plan so compelling that it would influence events in Sabino Canyon for nearly four decades.

The stream gauge constructed by Professor Woodward was a popular landmark for visitors to Sabino Canyon in the first decade of the twentieth century. *Courtesy Arizona Historical Society, Tucson: photo 62886, Upham Collection.*

While most others had planned small dams near the mouth of the canyon, Woodward proposed a huge structure at a completely new site, more than three miles farther upstream, where the canyon narrows abruptly to a spectacular, sheer-walled gorge. (The location is about a mile beyond the end of the present road in Upper Sabino Canyon.) Woodward quickly claimed the necessary water rights, surveyed the dam site, and soon had a gauge constructed to convince potential investors that the stream flow was adequate. In 1904 he moved on to another university, but by then others were committed to his plan. Two years later they formed the Great Western Power Company and bought out Woodward's interests in the project.

The new company's plans rapidly grew more ambitious. By 1907 they included not only a 300-foot concrete dam at Woodward's site in Sabino Canyon, to create a large reservoir, but a smaller dam and reservoir in nearby Bear Canyon as well. An elaborate system of pipes, aqueducts, generating stations, and transmission lines would supply both water and electric power to the city of Tucson and open up thousands of acres in the Tucson Basin to irrigation.

Professor Woodward's dam site. Had the dam been built, the point from which this photograph was taken would have been submerged when the reservoir was full.

ROADS TO THE PINE COUNTRY

At the turn of the century Tucsonans were already riding the rugged Sabino Canyon Trail (laid in 1896–1897) to camp, hunt, and escape the desert heat in the cool pine forests of the Santa Catalina Mountains. When the more direct Plate Rail Trail was finished in 1912, Tucsonans quickly adopted it as the new route of choice. A few years later John Knagge, together with his teenage sons Ed and Tom, took over a burro train serving the growing number of mountain cabins. The train became a traveling general store for vacationers in the Santa Catalina Mountains. The Knagges hauled families up the Plate Rail Trail at the end of May, kept them supplied all summer, then hauled them back down again at the end of August. They also carried provisions for miners, lumbermen, and forest rangers, and in December the braying burros trudged down Sabino Canyon loaded with Christmas trees.

The new trail was excellent, but travel on the back of a burro already seemed out-of-date to a populace that had become infatuated with the motorcar. In 1915 county voters approved a bond issue to build an automobile road up Sabino Canyon, but the project was delayed when a new estimate more than doubled its cost. Meanwhile, a road was completed up the north side of the Santa Catalinas in 1920, and Sabino Canyon's burro train fell victim to progress. In 1931 a new survey for a southern road was made. Surprisingly, the Sabino Canyon route, long assumed to be the best, was rejected in favor of one starting up the slope several miles to the east. Federal prisoners began laying the present Hitchcock Highway in 1933.

On the Sabino Canyon Trail, 1910.
Courtesy Arizona Historical Society, Tucson: photo 8821.

In 1910 laborers began tunneling through the massive rock wall at the Sabino Canyon dam site, so that the stream could be diverted while the dam was raised. The old Sabino Canyon Trail, winding back and forth across the creek, was not suitable for delivering men and heavy materials to the dam site, so the company built an entirely new route, called the Plate Rail Trail, high on the eastern canyon slope.

But while the men worked, the stream gauge was telling a discouraging story. An extreme drought had dried out the creek, and the charts showed that had the dam already existed, the reservoir would have been nearly empty. Plagued meanwhile by water rights disputes, the company collapsed.

Although the Great Western Power Company never built its dams, it left its mark on Sabino Canyon. By 1912 the Plate Rail Trail had been extended up the mountain and a telephone line had been strung beside it. Eventually, the route came to be called the Phoneline Trail. You can still see remnants of the poles and wire today. At the old dam site the uncompleted diversion tunnel penetrates 125 feet into the canyon wall, and heavy iron eye-bolts rust slowly where they were driven into stone by determined men many years ago.

An Old Idea Revived

In the two decades following the collapse of the Great Western Power Company there were several attempts to resurrect the Sabino Canyon dam, but it took the upheaval of the Great Depression, with its huge government relief projects, to bring Professor Woodward's idea back to life.

In 1933 the Tucson Chamber of Commerce began energetically advocating a federal dam at Woodward's site in order to boost the city's faltering economy. By this time Tucson had developed other sources of water and electricity, so in its new incarnation the dam would provide neither. What the city needed now, or so many believed, was tourists. The Chamber envisioned a great lake in Sabino Canyon, a recreationist's paradise with boating, fishing, camping, and cabins. Streamside camping and picnic grounds would be created downstream

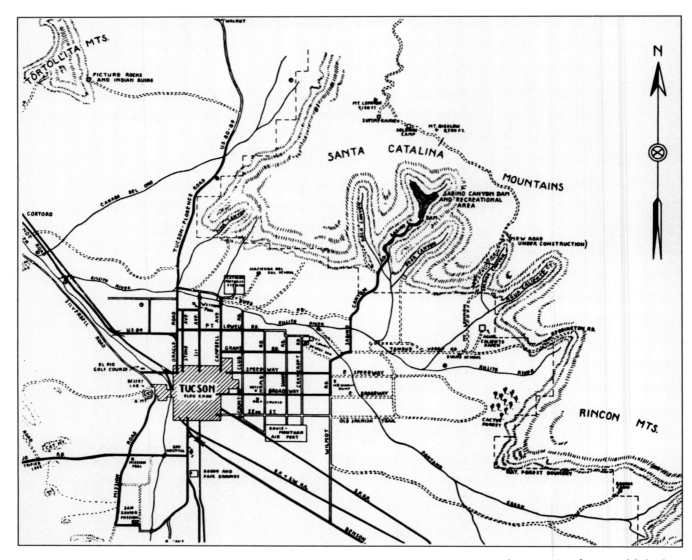

A promotional map published in 1936, prematurely showing the huge dam and reservoir that were never completed in Sabino Canyon. *Courtesy Arizona Historical Society, Tucson: map 678.*

along a picturesque access road. The route would cross the creek nine times over rustic stone bridges, each of which would also act as a small dam and form an inviting recreational pond.

In fall 1934 laborers for the Emergency Relief Administration, or ERA, began blasting out new roadbed beyond the old picnic grounds at Rattlesnake Canyon. The workers were homeless transients who had been uprooted by the nation's economic crisis and drawn to Tucson by its warm climate. Pleased to be doing productive work in beautiful surroundings, the men laid out two hundred yards of roadbed in the first week. Within a month, Tucsonans were applying to the Forest Service for lakeside cabin permits. The next year, after four bridges had been built, men from the Works Progress Administration took over. The Chamber of Commerce and the Sunshine Climate Club printed a map showing the "Sabino Canyon Dam and Recreation Area" as though they already existed. The route from the

The seventh bridge in Upper Sabino Canyon, nearing completion in 1936. *National Archives photo 69-NS-30160.*

city was surfaced so that Tucsonans would be able to drive to the lake entirely over paved roads. The last of the nine stone bridges was finished, and the road began climbing the eastern canyon wall in the final approach to the dam site.

But in their enthusiasm most Tucsonans were overlooking an essential fact: No funds had been allotted for construction of the dam itself.

In late summer 1936 the Army Corps of Engineers held a public hearing in Tucson to settle the fate of the Sabino Canyon Dam. The meeting room was packed. One after another, citizens and government officials testified unanimously in favor of the project. A month later the Corps issued its anxiously awaited report. It concluded with a recommendation that the dam be built, provided that "local interests are willing to contribute $500,000 toward the project." This last sentence was

Brass plaque on a bridge in Upper Sabino Canyon

the death knell for Pima County's greatest relief project. The county had offered to contribute only $600. Construction of the access road halted a mile short of the dam site.

We had almost lost Sabino Canyon. The Great Western Power Company's dam would have diverted the entire flow of Sabino Creek outside the canyon, drying up the stream and destroying its precious aquatic and riparian habitats. The effects of the Depression version of the dam would have been more insidious. By eliminating flooding and providing a nearly constant year-round discharge into the creek, it would have drastically disrupted the ecology of the riparian communities downstream. Fortunately for the future of Sabino Canyon, Professor Woodward's dam site was put out of reach of engineers when it was included in the Pusch Ridge Wilderness in 1978.

A New Recreation Area

The New Deal left more in Sabino Canyon than a road to nowhere. After the WPA took over the work in Upper Sabino Canyon, the ERA turned to building roads and campgrounds in Lower Sabino. Meanwhile, the Civilian Conservation Corps (CCC) had also been working on recreational facilities and had constructed a new ranger station just west of the canyon. In June 1937, after the demise of the great dam at Professor Woodward's site, the ERA's transient laborers began building a much less grandiose structure in Lower Sabino Canyon. The following spring two thousand Tucsonans turned out to hear the speeches at the dedication ceremony, held to the strains of a combined junior high school orchestra. It was far less than they had hoped for, but Sabino Canyon finally had a dam after all.

Anglers on the dam in Lower Sabino Canyon, 1939. *Courtesy Arizona Historical Society, Tucson: photo 7239.*

The tiny lake was instantly popular. The centerpiece of the new Sabino Canyon Recreation Area, it regularly filled with swimmers, and fisherman crowded the dam angling for stocked bass and sunfish. Today the lake has long since silted in, and only a shallow pond remains. Trees have grown up in the sand, and Sabino Lake is now a favorite destination for birdwatchers from around the country.

The 1930s saw the beginning of heavy use of Sabino Canyon. The number of visitors skyrocketed after World War II, as Tucson's population boomed. The Forest Service responded by building new facilities and closing the canyon at night, but it was not enough. On busy days the canyon walls rang with the sound of automobile horns, and the air reeked of exhaust.

The era of the private car in Sabino Canyon ended unexpectedly in 1973, when the canyon was temporarily closed to cars for repairs and improvements to facilities. Visitors walking or bicycling in smelled the clean air, heard the quiet, and urged

CAMP LIFE

Laborers employed by the Emergency Relief Administration during the Great Depression constructed many of the facilities we see today in Sabino Canyon. Life in their small camp in Upper Sabino was less than luxurious, but residents like Bill Griffin, grateful to be working during those difficult years, laughed at trying conditions. "Rain! . . . In some of the tents we had all of an inch of water on the floor and two inches on the beds with a continual promise of more to come. I was warned not to put my hand on the wet canvas as that would cause it to leak. Leak? I came dern near drowning—and I didn't touch the d——d canvas. It's fun to lie on one's bed and look up at the water streaming down the outside (and inside) of the tent, and to count the tadpoles and pollywogs, along with fish worms and wondering whether the next fish to slide down will be a trout or a perch" (*The Oasis,* October 11, 1935, Arizona Historical Society).

The Emergency Relief Administration camp in Upper Sabino Canyon, after wooden roofs had replaced the leaky canvas covers over the laborers' cabins. *Courtesy Coronado National Forest.*

the Forest Service to close the gates permanently to traffic. Others objected, and there were angry debates in the editorial pages of Tucson's newspapers. In the end the Forest Service compromised with a shuttlebus service. Since 1978, when the first shuttle ran in Sabino Canyon, the shuttle has itself become a popular tourist attraction.

Sabino Canyon's Future

For thousands of years Sabino Canyon offered precious food and water to hunter-gatherers and farmers. In the last century and a half Tucsonans have come to the canyon seeking ranch-land, water, electric power, and gold. Most recently we have sought the quiet pleasures of nature and a retreat from city life.

In the 1980s Tucson's expanding suburbs reached Sabino Canyon. On crowded weekends today, visitors may see more of each other than of wildlife. A century after city-dwellers began spreading their picnic cloths under the cottonwoods, Sabino Canyon faces the same uncertainties as popular natural areas throughout the country. Will we "love it to death"? Or will we preserve Tucson's oasis to delight and inspire us into the twenty-first century and beyond?

Children on a field trip to Sabino Canyon. *Courtesy Sabino Canyon Volunteer Naturalists.*

Afterword

As we approach the twenty-first century, there are many reasons to feel hopeful about Sabino Canyon's future. Enlightened management by Coronado National Forest has reduced many of the immediate threats posed to the canyon by its nearness to a growing city. Overnight camping is no longer allowed in the Sabino Canyon Recreation Area, and private cars have been eliminated. Regulations now forbid bringing pets into the canyon, harming or removing natural or cultural features, and, significantly, introducing exotic animals and plants. With an eye to the canyon's long-term preservation, the Sabino Canyon Volunteer Naturalists, a knowledgeable and dedicated group cooperating with the Santa Catalina Ranger District, offer educational and interpretive programs to thousands of children and adults every year.

Still, problems remain. Some exotic species already introduced continue to spread, altering native biotic communities. Nearby housing developments are probably interfering with the natural movements of some native wildlife to and from the canyon. House sparrows, free-roaming dogs, and feral cats, the animal hangers-on of suburban civilization, are now showing up in and near Lower Sabino Canyon.

Mid-winter moonrise

Nor is Sabino Canyon immune from forces affecting the entire region, even the globe. Increased ultraviolet radiation caused by stratospheric ozone depletion, possibly coupled with airborne pollution, is the suspected cause of a surface degeneration ("epidermal browning") affecting saguaros in Sabino Canyon and throughout their range. The same dual influences of ultraviolet light and air pollution may also be responsible for the almost complete disappearance of the lowland leopard frog from the Sabino Canyon Recreation Area — part of an apparent decline of amphibians around the world.

What will be the effects on the canyon of global warming? Of the removal of water from Sabino Creek by the mountain town of Summerhaven? Of soaring numbers of visitors? We must find the answers to questions like these if we are to pass on this beautiful place, so rich in history and blessed by natural diversity, to our children's children.

Further Reading

Alcock, John. *Sonoran Desert Spring*. Chicago: University of Chicago
     Press, 1985.
———. *Sonoran Desert Summer*. Tucson: University of Arizona Press,
     1990.
Alexander, Kathy. *Paradise Found*. Mt. Lemmon, Az.: Skunkworks
     Productions, 1991.
Bowden, Charles. *Frog Mountain Blues*. Tucson: University of
     Arizona Press, 1987.
Gregonis, Linda M., and Karl J. Reinhard. *Hohokam Indians of the
     Tucson Basin*. Tucson: University of Arizona Press, 1979.
Harte, John Bret. *Tucson: Portrait of a Desert Pueblo*. Woodland
     Hills, Ca.: Windsor Publications, 1980.
Krutch, Joseph Wood. *The Desert Year*. Tucson: University of
     Arizona Press, 1985.
———. *The Voice of the Desert: A Naturalist's Interpretation*. New
     York: William Morrow and Co., 1971.
Larson, Peggy. *The Deserts of the Southwest*. San Francisco: Sierra
     Club Books, 1977.
MacMahon, James A. *Deserts*. New York: Alfred A. Knopf, Inc.,
     1985.

Nabhan, Gary Paul. *Saguaro*. Tucson: Southwest Parks and
Monuments Association, 1986.

Olin, George. *House in the Sun*. Tucson: Southwest Parks and
Monuments Association, 1977.

Polzer, Charles W. et al. *Tucson: A Short History*. Tucson: Southwest
Mission Research Center, 1986.

Sonnischen, C. L. *Tucson: The Life and Times of an American City*.
Norman: University of Oklahoma Press, 1987.

Acknowledgments

The author sincerely thanks the following individuals and organizations for offering information and assistance in far too many ways to list here: Constance Altshuler, Robert Barnacastle, Robert Byars, Judith and Richard Edison, Paul R. Fish, R. Roy Johnson, John T. and Mary Knagge, Charles H. Lowe, Janet Miller, Walter B. Miller, Gale Monson, William Mueller, James Officer, Carl Olson, Yar Petryszyn, Tanner Pilley, Rodney Replogle, Edward Ronstadt, Millard Rowlette, Robert Scarborough, Cecil Schwalbe, Ronnie Sidner, Sharon Urban, Thomas and Rebecca Van Devender, Diana Warr; the Arizona Historical Society, in particular David Faust (Fort Lowell Museum), Barbara Bush, and Lori Davisson; Coronado National Forest, especially Mary Farrell, Isabelle Harrison, James McDonald, Meredith Penn, Steve Plevel, Deni Seymour, Thomas Skinner, Margaret Strong, Daniel and Stella Yurkievich; The Fenster School; Harbinger House; the Sabino Canyon Volunteer Naturalists, especially Mabel Bendixen, Yvonne Endrizzi, Juniata Hirsch, Brian Mathie, Norma Niblett, and Karen Nickey; the Tucson Audubon Society; the University of Arizona Library Special Collections and Map Collection.

My special gratitude to Cheryl and Catherine Lazaroff for their unwavering support, including many hours of assistance and companionship in the field. To my parents, Louis Lazaroff and Ethel Wentworth Lazaroff: Thank you for letting your young son raise tadpoles on the kitchen counter.

Index

Scientific names of selected plants and animals are given after the common names.

Italicized page numbers refer to maps, drawings, and photographs.

About the Author

DAVID WENTWORTH LAZAROFF became interested in nature as a boy exploring the hills and streams in his San Francisco Bay Area neighborhood. After working as a high school science teacher and later as an interpretive naturalist for the National Park Service, he moved to Tucson in 1977 to become an environmental education specialist with Coronado National Forest. He became fascinated by Sabino Canyon while developing an educational program for visiting schoolchildren and has continued to study and photograph the canyon since leaving the Forest Service in 1986. He is now an independent naturalist, writer, and photographer.

From the President's Desk

Protect, Preserve, and Enhance is the mission statement of Friends of Sabino Canyon (F.O.S.C.). Our outstanding track record of works in and around Sabino Canyon has brought in something to the tune of a million dollars in donated funds for trails and infrastructure, including the funding of busses for schools that can otherwise no longer afford educational school trips to the canyon. We reach out to our region in southern Arizona and beyond by properly equipping law enforcement with radios that can navigate the traitorous terrain and dangerous positions found in the surrounding mountains and wilderness. Our reputation is upheld with the Department of Agriculture, Forest Service.

So, too, we are proud to help David Lazaroff with the publication of his fine book, a book that is in demand and worthy of the attention. The book has broad strokes and in-depth details of a lifetime of knowledge obtained from his hands-on experience. I have known David for some time, and we don't always agree on all topics but if I where to relate it to a game, I would say he has won most of the rounds on those topics. But the common ground between us is the passion and respect we share for this gem called Sabino Canyon. I'm the new kid in town, looking for the top gun to prove my worth. David is the never-wavering, cool, calm, and collected sheriff. It's an honor to know him.

I would like to thank all my partners in the canyon, not the least of which is Sabino Canyon Volunteer Naturalists, for their plea of supporting this work. Thanks to my board of directors for unanimously funding the work, and to the community and donors of F.O.S.C. for allowing us to have the financial wherewithal to do the things we do. This book is no different; it is a wonderful example.

In a way, "protect, preserve, and enhance" could be a fine life model, one's mantra—a new way of looking into nature no matter where you live or visit, even if only for a day or two. To those of us that live and breathe this marvelous place called Sabino Canyon, David's book is mastery of the diversity that is so rare and, in some ways, fleeting.

Enjoy your book and the words, observations, and thoughts of the author, and the generosity of a passionate nonprofit that I am very proud to be a part of.

See you in the canyon,
David Bushell
President, Friends of Sabino Canyon